Rallying to Win

Rallying to Win

A COMPLETE GUIDE TO NORTH AMERICAN RALLYING

Jean Calvin

Bond/Parkhurst Books

ISBN: 978-0-393-60002-5

Library of Congress Card No. 73-86002

BOND/PARKHURST BOOKS, NEWPORT BEACH, CALIFORNIA

Printed in the United States of America

Contents

Foreword

WHEN WE STARTED our rally career way back when, there was only one book in print recognized as the oracle on the sport. It was *Rallies, Trials, and Gymkhanas* by Arthur Peck and David Hebb, still an excellent source of information. Over the years there have been several other books written on the American style of rallying, most of them paperbacks, some almost privately circulated.

For several years we dreamed of writing a modern rally book, one that would encompass the rapid growth of the computer age in the sport as well as all the basics of time-speed-distance work. We thought such a book might fill the gap between the paperback volumes of tables and systems and the "There-I-was" style hard-cover books on European rallying.

The sport has many aspects in this country, but most events bear at least some resemblance to one domestic style of rallying. (Only a relative few hard-core devotees have the interest, time and money to pursue the car-punishing, off-road and on, European type rallies.) Therefore we have devoted the bulk of

7

this book to time-speed-distance rallies, and we have divided the material into chapters covering all the various types of TSD rallies and the equipment required to be competitive.

Although we have spent years on the rally trails, we have no illusions about our expertise as a competitor. We have made all the mistakes more than once. We have in fact made both the common and the uncommon mistakes. So we can speak with a good deal of authority on how to go wrong on the rally route. However we have many friends who are expert rallyists, who win consistently and who all helped to make this book possible. In the course of our research we interviewed a great many men and women all over the country in an effort to present the most current aspects of the sport. We have every confidence that we have missed points that some readers might deem necessary in a rally book, but we have attempted to cover all the essential points that pertain to rallying in this country.

Beginner and gimmick-style events have been covered thoroughly because we feel those chapters are of value to many individuals and entire families who rally only occasionally and who are more than content with a simple contest that requires no special equipment for active participation.

The new Pro Series from SCCA has made the performance rally a must topic for any modern rally book, and we see this segment of the sport growing in popularity in the coming years. A good deal of space has been devoted to the SCCA National rules, primarily because they represent a national standard, and also because they are the basis for the only bona fide national championship available to U.S. rallyists. We have picked the brains of a good many experts in rallying to help us explain the traps and conventions that, quite frankly, we find perplexing at first glance. We think this information will prove valuable to the average rallyist on that day when he first encounters trickery in the general instructions.

We owe sincere thanks to numerous people in the rally sport whose ideas and suggestions contributed to the text. In particular we must thank some of the experts whom we quote at length, especially Russ Brown and Wayne Zitkus. We owe a considerable debt for help with the chapters on clocks and navigation systems to rally champions Ken and Bonney Adams, Fran and Don Edlund, and John and Judy Roache, whose knowledge and skill is the bedrock of our own information. Their patience through *hours* of explanations contributed mightily to the completion of the project.

We enjoy rallying today as much as we did when we first started in the sport. Although we have been involved in other forms of motor sport, we think rallying is the most fun of all, simply because anyone with a car can become an instant competitor. It is truly a participant sport and we think that is the reason rallying appeals to so many Americans: we are a sports-happy and car-crazy nation, and rallying offers a combination of these values. The book is intended to be useful as reference material, chapter by chapter, and we also planned it to be easily readable, cover to cover. We hope you find it that way.

—Jean Calvin

The American
Way of Rallying

THERE ARE SEVERAL meanings applied to the word rally, and our dictionary includes the political conclave, the gathering of strength, and also the automobile rally. It is the latter term that concerns us in this book, and the dictionary defines it as a long distance race held on public roads with numerous checkpoints along the route. That may be the one-world definition, but most rallyists in this country insist emphatically that a rally is not a race, and for the most part this is true. A car rally is quite basically a follow-the-leader event. The leader is the rallymaster; he has been over the designated route several times before the rally starts. The competition involves following that route *exactly*, with total accuracy in mileage and timing. The competitors do not have prior knowledge of the route, average speeds, or total distance involved. The only person who does know all this in advance is the rallymaster. The majority of U.S. rallies are a computation and route-following challenge; the average speeds quoted in the instructions will always be less than the legal speed limits. Each car runs in its own time slot, and scoring is done on the basis of timing accuracy through control points called checkpoints or controls.

There are many degrees of rally competition in this country ranging from the pure gimmick to the intricate national championship events. Almost all rallies are organized by some sort of car club, and it is the club members who rally and also provide the workers to man the control points, do the scoring, and lay out the event. The car club, often a sports car club, is the backbone of the sport of rallying. In fact it was the sports car clubs that founded the rally movement in this country.

Some enthusiasts may argue that the Glidden Tours at the turn of the century were the first U.S. rallies. Others just as staunchly proclaim that the Monte Carlo-type rally is the bedrock of the sport. In this book we are concerned with rallying today, in North America, and a bit of history is in order.

In 1937 the Automobile Racing Club of America staged what may well have been the first road rally in the USA. John C. Rueter wrote a book, *A.R.C.A.*, tracing the sports car movement before the Hitler war. In the book he tells about the Mount Washington Rally held in July of 1937. Four cars entered, and starting points were placed in both Boston and New York City. The rally was organized along European lines of the times, with pre-set time allowances between controls, but there were also some hidden controls where early arrival carried a heavy penalty. The event started on Saturday afternoon, ran through the night, and finished at the starting line for the Climb to the Clouds hillclimb staged on the Mount Washington Carriage Road in New Hampshire. Three teams were official finishers in the rally, won by Mr. and Mrs. Edward Dane who started from Boston in a BSA. ARCA organized more rallies in the 1930s and some attracted upwards of 20 entries. However World War II put a stop to automotive competition in general, and the rally changed a good deal in the post-war era. We like to think that the Mount Washington event was the first American rally: it followed the format of international rallying but with some local options. And that is how the sport evolved in the U.S.

The domestic rally has truly separated from all other forms of competition for a variety of reasons. The type of event which is a thinly disguised road race is extremely rare, confined to those parts of the country where population is sparse and law enforcement agencies cooperative. Most rallies today are not races at all, for a number of reasons. First is The Law. One does not race on public roads and stay out of trouble with The Law. Second, the rally car is usually the owner's daily transportation as well, and insurance companies take a dim view of anything that smacks of racing, especially on cars already equipped with a sporting image and high premiums. Nonetheless, there is a good deal of excitement and keen competition in the rally world. The proliferation of foreign and domestic cars bearing rally stripes and rally packs is some testimony to the popularity of this virtually unsung sport. We know it is an unheralded sport, for there is little of rallying in enthusiast magazines, nor will an event chairman find much help or sponsorship from the auto accessory people. The news media and the manufacturers generally dismiss any inquiry with the statement that rallying is a Sunday afternoon drive, "of no interest to us." Well gang, golf was a participant sport too, and very light on news value, until TV discovered golf, and sponsors now flock to the events, the sportsmen, and the products.

Rallying didn't really get under way in America until after World War II. It was brought to life by the sports car crowd who were buying MGs and Jaguars as fast as the British could ship them over on the boat. The rally world actually began organizing on the east coast, and events ranged from Sunday tours to some pretty hairy European-style bashes. Marque sports car clubs and the fledgling Sports Car Club of America were the sponsors of the events, and as the cars spread westward so did the clubs. In those days many major companies sponsored employee car clubs too. Perhaps the most famous example nationwide was the Lockheed Sports Car Club who were justly famed for their 24-hour enduro rally across the southern California desert.

In the 1940s and well into the 1950s, little-used roads were easy to find, and high speed stages, impossible average speeds in the mountains, and similar performance ploys were coupled with the time, speed, and distance work on the better known rallies. As the rally movement spread across the country, the population and traffic density also increased. By the 1960s it became difficult to organize a performance style rally with any reasonable degree of safety for either participants or innocent bystanders, except in a few isolated sectors of the nation. Plus the increasing awareness by police of the sport of rallying often meant there was no security from arrest, whether for real offenses or for trivial things such as the placement of a checkpoint. With these problems facing rallymasters in major urban areas, they turned to careful calculation of average speeds and distance problems to make the rally more interesting. Tricky course finding, and craftily written instructions were incorporated into the format, and these factors have been developed to near ultimate powers today. As a result, the present state of the art can be very perplexing to the casual observer.

Although we will touch on gimmick and European style rallies in this book, we are primarily concerned with the navigational rally. The nav rally has been described as many things, but it is actually a contest where the rally team tries to duplicate the rallymaster's progress over a pre-determined course. The team that most accurately follows the route through a series of time controls and matches the average speeds called out in the instructions is the winner. The instructions given to each rally team will describe the route and indicate the average speeds to be maintained along the way. The work involves following the route through all its twists and turns, clued by the signs and mileages given in the instructions, and accurately maintaining the required average speeds. The navigator/passenger is involved in calculations necessary to translate the average speed quoted in the instructions into an elapsed time which will match the mileage clicking out on the car's odometer—hence the usual description of a navigational rally as a time-speed-distance, or TSD, event.

The nav or TSD rally can be a simple beginner-style run of two or three hours, covering less than 100 miles, or it can be like the exacting, two day, 400-mile-plus events that qualify as the Sports Car Club of America's National Championship series. In between these extremes, the bulk of TSD rallies are run on Saturday or Sunday, cover about 150 miles, and take about six or seven hours with a lunch break and a gas stop. This type of rally can be a club event, simple in design and mostly for fun, or it can be a regional, city, or state championship with the most trying problems one could encounter anywhere. There are numerous events in all corners of the country, and there is scarcely an area that doesn't contain at least one rally club. We know for a fact that there are at least a dozen rallies every weekend of the year in the Los Angeles area, so there must be literally hundreds of events every Sunday all over the country. That adds up to a lot of people involved in this off-beat breed of automotive competition.

We have often been asked, "What type of person rallies?" That is about the same as asking what type of person drives a car. Rally folk come from all walks of life today, and they seemingly share few interests besides the sport. A Sunday rally might see teenagers and their parents competing; age, young or old, is no barrier to success in this sport. At one time many people thought that the navigator at least had to have special skills, primarily in mathematics. Rallying is a mental game as well as a test of driving ability, but the math problems actually seldom exceed eighth-grade levels. With today's calculators and navigational aids, the ability to run a slide rule in a moving car is no longer a requirement for the navigator. As a rule the rally team can be no more than two people, but mixed couples or all-male/all-female teams are common. The professional rallies at the top end of the sport lean heavily to all-male teams, at least in recent years. In fact the SCCA National Champions lately have been pairs of men. This trend for the SCCA title is probably related to economics. National rallies are held all over the country, and the travelling expenses plus the expenses of the rally itself take big chunks out of the purse for accommodations, food, and gasoline. It becomes more practical to shoot for the national points if more than one family income is involved.

The weekend rally, however, is heavily peopled with mixed couples; many a casual date has evolved to a rally-winning team, and even to marriage. In most cases the man drives and his feminine companion inherits the navigation chores. Remember, rallying is a team sport, and this fact will become more evident as we go into the details of dividing the duties in competition. Each team develops its own operating procedures as they progress in skill. Generally, the driver is responsible for staying

15

on course, spotting signs, and so forth. He is clued by directions, mileages, and time signals from the navigator, who may spend the entire rally with head buried in maps, charts, calculators, and timing devices. We know some navigators who never see the scenery on a rally and communicate with the driver in terms and tones exclusive to the competition. Conversation comes only at the lunch break and in the dead time at a control. Those people are really serious competitors—most teams do not develop such fierce spirit. The average winning team will enjoy the rally enough to digress from the business at hand occasionally, often to laugh at a mistake just recently made and more recently evident. Like arriving at a control with a calculated perfect score of zero, only to find it is an off-course control and good for 100 penalty points. Blah!

Every rally type we know seems to have a slightly different idea about what the sport does for him. Perhaps this is what makes rallying such a fascinating type of recreation for such a wide variety of people. In the typical Sunday rally entry you may find every type of person in town, a veritable cross section of America. Their common denominator is enthusiasm for automobiles and rallying. The average rally driver is not a frustrated racer, as many might think. More often he is proud of his own brand of performance driving—rally driving—and he works hard to improve his skills. Some people buy a particular brand of car because of its rally capabilities; others get into the rally game because they own a sporty car and want to do something besides polish it on weekends. Although, as we shall see, one can spend a goodly bit of money on rally equipment, it takes next to nothing to get started in the sport. That factor is one good reason for the steady growth of rallying as practiced in America.

On the first-ever rally, one needs nothing more than a car, a few dollars for the entry fee, a full tank of gas, a pencil and paper, and some sort of timepiece. A clipboard for the navigator is handy, but a cardboard backed notebook is more than adequate. We always recommend more than one pencil or pen, since these items are apt to roll under the seat when dropped and it is handy to have a replacement ready. The watch can be anything that counts time: a wrist watch will do fine. It is nice to have a sweep second hand, but for the first few events the

Timex or whatever is available will serve very well. Naturally the car should be in reasonable mechanical shape, but it can be anything—a truck, a monster sedan, or a nimble sport sedan— whatever happens to be in the driveway, so long as it is street legal. The driver must have a state operator's license, and some clubs require proof of public liability insurance, but that is seldom a habit on local events.

Club events frequently have some vague advance publicity, and it shouldn't be too difficult for the neophyte rallyist to find an event. Unfortunately, most car clubs are not listed in telephone books; they usually exist in some post office box. City newspapers list motor sports events once or twice a week, either in the sports section or in the classified ad section where they list used sports cars. It can be called anything from *Pit Stop* to *Coming Event Calendar*. Listings include club races, rallies, slaloms, and so forth, and dates and a phone number for additional information are provided. This is the easiest method of finding a rally.

If your newspaper doesn't include this service, you'll have to do a bit of detective work. Contact the SCCA National headquarters in Denver to find the closest SCCA region and thus find a rally club. SCCA has over 100 regions so there is one within reach of almost every potential rallyist. If one wants faster action than the mail can provide, there are other methods of finding a car club to lead into a rally event. Many dealers in imported cars maintain a bulletin board in the agency that lists upcoming events for their cars, and quite a few dealers, domestic and foreign iron, have a resident car club. Ford, Chevrolet (Corvette), and Datsun dealers are the most prominent in club sponsorship, and even if your car is another breed, the local dealer of those makes is a good source for rally information.

If you are still out on a limb (although it is hard to believe you haven't found a rally yet) try finding a car club, any car club, even if it is concerned with another type of sport like drag racing. In smaller towns most car clubs are aware of each other, even though their interests are not the same. The drag strip may also serve as a slalom course and a staging area for rallies. Ask around and you will undoubtedly uncover kindred spirits who may even be your neighbors.

Although rallying was originally a sport for the sports car set, it is now practiced in all types of vehicles. (The International Championship Press on Regardless Rally in Michigan in 1972 was won by a Jeep Wagoneer.) In the '50s, rally competition was still thought of as something people did with sports cars.

Some folks even thought an open roadster was required to be eligible to rally, but the advent of compact cars and pony cars from Detroit and high performance sedans from overseas changed that idea to almost a complete reversal. Additionally the idea of a rally has been adapted to other types of vehicles in their own bailiwicks. Rallies occur for motorcycles, snow-mobiles, four-wheel-drive vehicles, dune buggies, even airplanes. The scope is endless. This book will not attempt to be all things to all manner of rally people. We will confine our interest to the road rally for street licensed automobiles, and the common expression of that type of rally is the time-speed-distance event.

*Novice Rallying
& the
Seat-of-the-Pants
Class*

YOUR FIRST RALLY can be great fun or a big disappointment. It certainly helps if you have some idea of the nature of the sport before sallying forth on a navigational rally. Once you have located an event, be sure it is a beginner-style rally, or that at least it includes a beginner or novice class or a seat-of-the-pants class. It is not practical to start your rally career on a championship run, where the course-following and time-keeping problems are designed for the experts. These problems could turn you off from rallying before you get started. We know of a championship rally held a few years back where half the field (including us) got lost on the odometer leg, the first leg of the rally, which traditionally should hold no course-following problems. That type of experience is discouraging. The first-time rally team will enjoy it all much more if the rally is geared to all levels of skill.

The first rule in any kind of rallying is to stay on course. The most elaborate instrumentation in the world will not help you if you miss a turn and wander off the route. Some gadgetry can help you recover your calculations once you're back on course (we'll go into that later), but the big clue is to stay on the rallymaster's route. We highly recommend to all beginners that they concentrate on that segment of the instructions. Few beginner rallies will contain tricky timed turns or mileage turns on the route; they are generally put together to point out a few course-following problems at a time, not the whole spectrum of traps in one event. We advise the beginner to use his watch only for pauses (add times) and for timing himself in and out on each leg. Learn the rules of the game before worrying about average speed. The novice rallyist will learn little about the sport if he runs on the right average speed but has lost the course.

A few general hints will make the first rally more enjoyable. First of all, locate the starting point, often a parking lot of a business which will be closed at the hour of departure. Be early, and once you have located the start, then go to a nearby gas station and fill the car with fuel, check under the hood, and be sure the tire pressures are right. It helps to do a super job cleaning the windshield and all glass. Finally, be sure both team members visit the rest room, because the starting point rarely has such facilities open at rally time. If the rally is a night event, be sure to carry extra batteries for the flashlight, or even an extra flashlight. Have the pencils, paper, and something to write on handy. Bring some sort of device that can be read in time of day: a wrist watch is fine. Now you are ready to check into the rally.

Go to the registration table, pay the entry fee, and sign the forms. Designate your class: beginner, novice, junior, or whatever is customary. You will be given the general instructions, a car number, and probably a dash plaque or some souvenir of the event. Somewhere around the registration table will be a master time watch; check your timepiece against it. The master time will be right on with WWV (the National Bureau of Standards radio station), and that time is the preferred reference in any rally.

Now go back to your car and put the car number in the place required, usually the lower portion of the right side of the windshield. Masking tape for this purpose is generally available at the registration desk. Start reading through the general

instructions. If you have read this book through before your first rally, you will have some idea of what these instructions mean. They are important. Be sure both driver and navigator read the general instructions completely, for there will undoubtedly be phrases that you don't understand. A Friday night rally generally provides a few expert rallyists to answer beginners' questions before the start. These people will no doubt be competing as well, since the pros often use a Friday-nighter to get in shape for a big event or to test some new gadget they have put in their car. Some sponsoring clubs actually have a few experts on hand just to answer questions. One beginner series we know of gives all beginner entries a middle-range starting number, and conducts a short driver's meeting for this section of the entry. Basically the driver's meeting is an explanation of the general instructions, and if your first rally provides this service, it is the ideal way to get started in the game.

Don't be afraid to ask questions, but don't pressure people whose starting number is coming up soon. You should have the answers before that happens if you arrived early. The route instructions will be delivered to your car several minutes before your out-time on most rallies, but a beginner event might pass out the route instructions with the generals to give the novice teams plenty of time to look at everything and ask questions. When you get the route instructions, be sure you have all the pages. Read through the odometer leg at least, because it will require the first few route instructions on the course. There will be no time controls within the odo leg, but you will have to follow the route instructions and you will be given a stipulated amount of time to cover the distance. However, there will be nothing tricky on the odo leg. On the rally proper, divide the duties so that the driver looks for signs and landmarks, and the navigator reads both the route instructions and the general instructions, and he helps spot the signs as well. Since most beginner rallies are run in the night, this system works the best until the rally team learns the tricks of staying on course.

You now have about ten minutes to go until your out-time. Locate the cars with numbers just ahead and behind you, and it doesn't hurt to note some distinguishing feature of these cars like make, paint, or license number. If you do get off course, or think you are, the sight of one of your starting neighbors can bring relief from panic. However, never rely on another rally car as a course-following or time-keeping gesture. You must run your own rally, because your neighbors could be lost or off rally time also. Still, on the first event, it is really comforting to see a familiar car, and it does inspire confidence in your most recent, questionable decision on a turn. The rally will have a man roaming the parking lot, and he will call your car number when it is time to get in line. Before you know it you will be at the out-marker. A starter will give you a countdown, and check this against your watch to be sure your timepiece is close to official time. If you have a trip odometer, zero it at the out-marker. If you don't have a trip odometer, write down your total odometer mileage. The starter will give you a signal to leave, but you need not burn rubber out of the parking lot. You are on an elapsed-time leg, and the allowance is normally quite generous. Once under way, relax and try to concentrate both pairs of eyes and both minds on staying on course.

Follow the instructions to the end of the odometer check, and note your mileage every time the instructions list a reference. Remember, you can arrive at the end of the odo leg early without penalty, but a late arrival will make you late starting on the first TSD leg. The odo check run should allow plenty of time for traffic, and you should arrive at the mark indicated in the route instructions with a few minutes to spare. Stop briefly at the mark, write down your mileage, and zero the trip odo. Go park until your out-time. To figure your out-time, add the elapsed time of the odo check, say 30 minutes, to your original out-time on the control card, say 9:20, and your out-time from the odo check will be 9:50. You can also figure your odometer correction factor by dividing your car's odometer reading by the official mileage. If you read less than the official figure, your factor will be in the 0.9 area. If you read more than official miles (which is far more common) your factor will be 1.01 or something similar. If you were trying to calculate TSD on this rally, you would need this factor in order to figure your true mileage against time. For your first event the factor gives you some indication of whether your odo is slow (less than official miles) or fast (more than official miles). You might try driving a little faster or slower on your speedo in order to get closer to the actual required average speed.

When your time comes up to leave the odo check, you will

probably be following the same car you followed at the start: few cars miss the odo check. Don't leave the area too early, because the first checkpoint could be around the next corner. If the out-speed (given in the average speed column of the route instructions) is 35 miles per hour or more, leave enough seconds early to get on time in half a mile. You are rallying by the seat of your pants now, so follow the route instructions carefully and leave the maintaining of the average speed to driver instinct, knowledge of the car, and luck. Remember that you don't have to break the law to make up lost time. The time penalty in points is the same whether you are early or late at a control, and generally anything over three minutes in either direction will bring the maximum point penalty. More than five minutes error will usually cost you a missed-checkpoint penalty (MCP). Check off each route instruction as you complete it, not before. The early checkoff of an instruction can be confusing in a maze situation, for instance, where your route instructions are rights and lefts with no landmark references. Keep your eyes peeled for signs that are eligible on the rally, and the navigator should keep reading the operative route instruction to the driver on long legs. You will feel a great sense of relief when you arrive at the first checkpoint, and feel even better when you discover it is actually the first checkpoint and you haven't missed a control.

The average beginner rally has three or four controls, and one of them will probably be a Do-It-Yourself type, so check the general instructions to find out how to do that operation. When you reach the last checkpoint, you will receive instruction to find the finish area, usually a restaurant, pizza parlor, bowling alley, and so forth. You can get refreshments to aid you while figuring out the score. Most novice rallies use the in-the-car control card, and that puts the responsibility of figuring the score on the individual competitor. Your in-time is marked over the out-time on each leg and you must subtract these time-of-day figures to find out your leg time. At the finish, the true times and the critique on the rally will be supplied or posted on the wall. Copy the true times onto your card and subtract to find the difference between true time and your time. The difference is your error on the leg. When you get that math done, add up all the error times, disregarding whether they are early or late, and you have your total error which is your score for the rally. If you are in doubt about subtracting hundredths of a minute, minutes, and hours, have one of the resident experts check your card before you turn it in to the scoring desk. If you have some beginner's luck you may be in line for a trophy, and if so, the club scoring team will also check your figures. Try to be accurate because a mistake in math could cost you a trophy. On a big event, the club will re-score only those cards with low points in each class. An average Friday night rally will have 60 to 90 cars; it is impossible to score that many cars on the spot unless the contestants do the initial work. You may wonder why you have a big (bad) score on one leg and a tiny (good) score on the next when you don't remember doing anything special on either one. Chances are you fell into a trap, a course instruction designed to put the unwary rallyist on a goof loop. Misinterpreting a trap instruction can range from not observing a misspelled word to using a sign on the wrong side of the street to trigger the action. This confusion is manufactured on purpose by the rallymaster. For example a spelling trap might read "Right at Wolffe Ave." on your route instructions, and the street sign would read "Wolfe Ave." Another example would be "Change speed to 45 mph at Main," and the first sign reading Main you see would be on the left side of the road, but the general instructions have told you that all signs used on the rally are on the right. Either trap would add running time to your score, and could lead you full circle around the block into an off-course control. Or it might just lead you around the block to add that time to your score. Generally there is a control right after a goof loop so that there is no opportunity to make up time lost. On most TSD rallies all time stops at the control, so time lost on one leg is gone forever and cannot be made up on the next leg. This factor will discourage entrants from speeding; the maximum penalty of say 300 points or three minutes on any leg is for the same purpose.

TSD rallies are really mind-bending exercises, and nearly all of them have some sort of trap based on clues hidden in the general instructions. The beginner will be wise to learn how to digest the general instructions and stay on course before he considers buying navigational gadgets. After a few short rallies, the novice team should try a full-day event, and still run without equipment, unless the budget permits the purchase of a stop watch. A stop watch can be a help to any rally team, no matter what direction they go eventually on equipment. The stop watch will make it easier for the navigator to figure elapsed time sections, transit zones, add-times, and the like. However, the time-of-day watch, even if it is a wrist watch, is a must in order to calculate out-times. By all means get into the all-day rally, and try a local championship event. Run in seat-of-the-pants class if there is no beginner class on the rally. A major event of this nature will present more and different challenges, and you may find several unnumbered instructions (called notes) working at the same time as a route instruction. In fact they may appear to conflict. You must check the general instructions for proper precedence, and try to follow the course through a succession of traps. Don't worry about figuring the TSD stuff now, just try to stay on the course and you will be amazed at your good scores. If you use the same car for each rally, you will soon learn how to gauge what the speedometer reads, and you will also learn how to figure the time lost at stop signs, and similar slow-down problems. As you grow more proficient, the navigator can calculate the time lost and the speed needed to regain such time just by using the stop watch, all that is allowed in most SOP classes. For the time being, just guess at it, and, when you feel confident in course-following, most of the time anyhow, then and only then are you ready to start TSD figuring seriously.

The step toward a nav rally class might be taken at this point, or you might decide to stay in an unequipped class, and work on getting to be a consistent winner. If you continue to run SOP, there are a number of nav aids you may or may not be able to use. In some parts of the country you may be allowed the use of a single odometer, rally tables, and factor cards; if so, look for tips on those things in the next chapter. The SOP rally winner faces a different type of challenge from that of the computer man. The expert nav types, usually, have the navigator heavily involved in running all the gadgets, and so leave all the course-finding and application of general instructions to the driver. Although all the calculating is done automatically, the navigator must still make a log so they can get back on course from a goof loop. The SOP team has the advantage of having two sets of eyes looking for signs, and two minds studying the GIs and the route instructions. SOP teams tend to be more relaxed in the rally, and often beat the best of the equipped cars in overall score on a tough trap rally. The timing contest rally, that with several speed changes per mile, will normally see the equipped car do the best on score. The SOP team can use any number of watches, and some teams use at least three: one for up-time (time ahead of the average speed), one for down-time (time behind average speed), and one for back-up and add times. They also use a log, with time noted at every speed change.

The SOP team will run without benefit of a mileage counter. At the odo check, the car's odometer error will be checked against the rallymaster's mile, and then the odo will be taped over. It does help to have an accurate speedo going in. Take the rally car to a speedometer shop and get it geared properly to provide a reading very close to the statute mile using the tires that will be used for rallying. This is a one-time operation, unless you change tire sizes. If you can't find a speedo shop, ask the local taxi driver or policeman for the name of the shop that does speedo calibrations. The driver should know how to read his speedo, and know that to do an actual 35 mph he must run an indicated 37 mph for example. After the odo check, the navigator can figure up a speedo correction chart on scratch paper for the speeds listed in the average speed column of the route instructions.

The SOP navigator must learn how to use the stop watch to figure lost time or gained time on the fly. There will always be moments when the rally car is running early, and more occasions when the rally car is running late. It isn't too difficult to stay close to the average required on the open road, but if you encounter a traffic jam, a stop sign, or anything that causes you to slow from the average speed, you must calculate the lost time, and also the time needed to get back on the average. It gets tricky without a odometer reading: you have to figure the percentages. Here is one method of doing it that works well.

Using the stop watch, say if the average speed is 50 mph, you start the watch when the car decelerates to 25 mph and let it run through the stop until the car accelerates back to 25 mph, then stop it. The watch reading is figured as the time lost in the stop. Most teams figure that the time is lost at 50 percent of the quoted speed. Usually the stop light will include an add-time on the instructions, so you compare your watch time with the add-time, wait out any differences, and start up again on time. If there is no add-time, or if the stop is not expected on the rally, the navigator must then figure the lost time on the watch as late, figure how much time they should run at a speed higher than the average to get back on time, again using a percentage factor. The navigator must keep a log of all times, and should note times at each speed change. Each SOP team will eventually work out a style of log that gets the job done for them.

This is truly seat-of-the-pants driving. A good team develops an instinct for just how much time can be gained or lost in certain situations in their car. It takes a good deal of practice, and a lot of ball-park figuring before a workable system develops, but some Class C cars post remarkable scores in rallying without an odometer. Naturally, the SOP car is apt to have much more error on long rally legs than on a succession of short legs, where they start clean every few miles. And as with all forms of rally work, the top SOP team does not come into being overnight. The winners work through many rallies to perfect their system. One good reason for staying in SOP class for championship rallying is quite simple: you need no expensive equipment to be successful. A year or so spent in SOP class is great fun and builds a fantastic background in course-following for the rally team that might want to move into an equipped class. Running SOP is the best possible discipline for learning how to stay on the course and follow the route without error. It is so difficult to figure the time lost on a leg when you have been off-course, that you soon learn to stop and look at signs before carrying on. If you do stay on course, you stand a good chance to win a trophy on any rally. SOP rally driving and navigating will teach you all the course-following tricks.

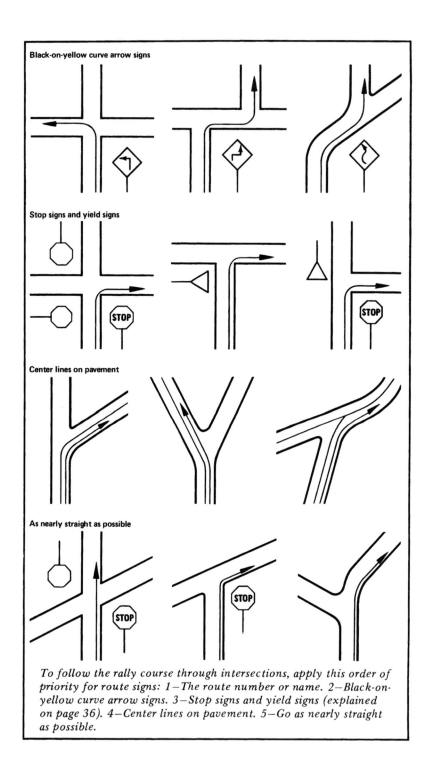

Black-on-yellow curve arrow signs

Stop signs and yield signs

Center lines on pavement

As nearly straight as possible

To follow the rally course through intersections, apply this order of priority for route signs: 1—The route number or name. 2—Black-on-yellow curve arrow signs. 3—Stop signs and yield signs (explained on page 36). 4—Center lines on pavement. 5—Go as nearly straight as possible.

30

The Fine Art of the Navigational Rally

IT IS INEVITABLE that the rally team will move into championship events. We must assume that the rally team is no longer in the beginner class, and they have learned to stay on course fairly well. They may be thinking about championship points, and must decide about class. Excluding those who prefer to stay in Class C, or SOP, it is also inevitable that the team will begin to acquire equipment and must choose between Class B with limited navigation aids and Class A where full blown computers are part of the scene. Personally we think it is just as difficult to do well in Class B as it is in Class A. The major difference between the operation in these two classes is the cost of the equipment.

Basically Class B will entail navigation from speed change to speed change with an accurate log being a must. Your calculating devices and watches may be reasonable in cost since your method of navigation calls for zero time and miles at each speed change, or perhaps zero time and miles at each checkpoint if your navigator is really adept at math. Class A allows the use of cumulative counting devices which provide leg-by-leg navigation and you can work on either elapsed time, time of day, or some combination of the two. The Class B car can be fully equipped with a circular slide rule device, the Stevens for example, factor cards, and a tenths-counting odometer for well under 100 bucks. Add stop watches and so on according to your taste and budget. All of this equipment is easy to find and available over the counter at rally stores or by mail order. For Class A rallying, the minimum in equipment would be a cumulative calculator like a Curta, factor tables, and dual odometers with their gear drive and cable. The cost is about $300 over the counter at retail, plus whatever timepieces you need or desire. A computer can cost anywhere from $400 for the basic unit to about $1000 for the complete set up, including electric clocks, driver readout, and the bag of gadgets. Individual use and value of all this type of equipment is covered in other chapters, so the choice is predicated on the budget primarily and, for either class, on one's dedication to the sport.

Nonetheless, equipment alone does not make a rally winner, and the game gets even more involved in the championship classes. ADVICE: Wait until you have won a few trophies in local events, entered a few local-council championship bashes, and have run in at least one SCCA national rally out of your home area before you reach a decision on equipment. Keep running SOP until you learn the game. Championship rallying is a tough and serious game, and it may not appeal to the team as a long range activity at this level. Find that out before you spend big bucks for equipment.

Major rallies run a number of involved problems concurrently, and the challenge is not only to stay on the course and keep accurate time-speed-distance records, but to enjoy this type of activity. Some may find that the deadly serious atmosphere of championship rallying makes these events no longer fun for them, but more like work. Others enjoy the most difficult rally course—find it relaxing. For them, serious rallying is recreation from their daily work. And there are still others who treat championship rallying as work, as a job, even though they may not have been competing in sponsored cars. This latter category includes some former SCCA National Champions. Those titles cost some couples dearly, even to the point of divorce. We don't think any amateur sport is worth that kind of strain or frustration. The problems on the rally course are either your kind of fun or they are not.

Properly forewarned then, let's find out how a navigation rally works.

Even granting that you are now ready for the big time, be prepared to make some giant errors on your first few major events. An SCCA National Rally, if it is a timing contest with several minute speed changes per mile, will be far beyond your SOP capabilities to score a zero, except by luck.

A trap rally may not have serious timing problems, but the simple-appearing instructions will contain some nifty traps to speed you off-course. Here is an example of a sequence of instructions that could be your downfall on score. The general instructions state that a SIGNAL is the joining of two or more eligible rally roads at which your travel is intended to be controlled by at least one standard red, amber, and green traffic signal, working or not. The key words are "eligible" and "working or not." Further the generals state that all roads are through, paved, and public so a signal controlling a plant entrance or any private road or parking area is not eligible. OK. The rally situation is this: you have a NOTE working that tells you to pause (add) 20 seconds at each SIGNAL. Because SIGNAL is not in quotation marks you know that it is an intersection controlled by a traffic signal on eligible rally roads, in other words a landmark rather than a sign. Now, the next numbered instruction is a speed change to 28 after the second "SPEED LIMIT 35," and the numbered instruction after that is a speed change to 31 at "1¼ minutes after previously executed instruction." The third numbered instruction says "left at SIGNAL." It all looks simple as you read it, but NOTES are defined in the generals as an instruction. OK, the problem looks to be finding the right signal to trigger the left turn. You change speed to 28 at the proper sign "SPEED LIMIT 35" and start a stop watch. At 50 seconds you come to an intersection controlled by a signal which activates the note for a 20-second add-time. This gives you 70 seconds after the signal, so you can't turn left: according to the previous instruction it is too early.

However, you might want to change speed to 31 when the

watch reads 75 seconds, but that is the trap and it is wrong. The numbered instruction said to change to 31 mph 1¼ minutes after previously executed instruction, and the note was an instruction. So, when you add in the 20 seconds for the first signal, at 70 seconds, you then restart the countdown for the 1¼ minutes. In the rally used for example, it all kept working through a series of signals for add-times that kept the countdown in a constant state of restart. You never did change to 31 mph or turn left, but carried on right into a control. If you did take a left, the subsequent instruction took you on a two-minute goof loop before sending you into the same control. Both routes were contained in just a few city blocks.

Another trap is an instruction that says to decrease your speed by 50 percent, and then one that says to increase speed by 50 percent. You are traveling at 36 mph and you decrease your speed to 18 mph. So far so good: 18 is 50 percent of 36. However, at the instruction to increase speed by 50 percent, the unwary just go back to 36 mph, which is wrong. The proper speed is 27 mph. Those dirty rats, or words to that effect. Many simple math problems do not seem simple in the car.

The rallymaster will try to arrange numbered instructions or notes so that it is difficult to figure out the traps in advance. It is common to see a NOTE telling one to increase speed by 5 percent at each "No Parking" or something similar, and sprinkled among the no parking signs will be a few numbered instructions containing average speed changes, so the correct average speeds have to be calculated at the point of action. There are countless variations of this type of trap. It seldom leads off-course, but it does produce the sight of a number of rally cars all going down the same road at a variety of average speeds, each team confident of being on the right speed.

Off-course traps are common in championship rallies; they are generally looped back to the course or controlled by an off-course checkpoint. The numerous situations that trigger these traps would fill an encyclopedia, but there are a few in universal use around the country. Like the spelling trap. The spelling trap is a favorite with all rallymasters, and they are not at all squeamish about making and posting their own signs with a misspelled word, or writing a misspelled word into the route instructions. Another is the restricted sign bit. The general instructions will state that "all quoted signs will be on the right or overhead unless otherwise instructed." OK, that takes care of any sign written in quotation marks. Now: "Other signs and all landmarks may be located anywhere." That blows it wide open. A sign used for an instruction, as long as it is not contained in quotes, can be right, left, overhead, or parallel to your line of travel. A succession of instructions with the sign in quotes will lull you into looking only to the right or overhead. Then—the next numbered instruction (simple but deceptive) is "Change speed to 45 at MERGING TRAFFIC." What harm could there be in that? Well, there are no quotes around MERGING TRAFFIC, and the sign is on the left. A mile or so down the road on the right you find another MERGING TRAFFIC, so you now have a time error for the distance you traveled at the wrong average speed. He did it to you again.

Standard practice calls for the execution of each numbered instruction before moving on to the next, but notes can come between without cancelling numbered instructions. However, in the sequence of instructions there can be some overlap between route instructions (turns) and speed-change instructions. A speed change may apply over a distance that spans a subsequent numbered instruction. Here is an example from the 1971 Andiamo National Rally.

Instruction: 41. CAST 30 mph at "SUKTIZ" for 1.00 mile
          42. Left after "GIRLS" on 23
          43. Right at "WOMEN"

The tricky part here is that you may or may not have run the 1.00 mile at 30 mph before you have to execute instructions 42 and 43. Instruction 41 has you change speed to 30 mph at (a sign) "SUKTIZ," then *one mile later, change back to your former speed,* or to a new speed, if one is given at that point. Instruction 42 says as soon as you have passed "SUKTIZ," look for "GIRLS." After passing it, turn left onto 23 at the first opportunity. Instruction 43 says that as soon as you have turned left onto 23 you stay on 23, looking for an opportunity to turn right at "WOMEN." When you do, you still may not have completed the 1.00 mile of the first instruction. You will worry.

A really keen trap which is popular in the midwest is the protected-road confidence game. A protected road is one that is controlled by a stop or yield sign; it triggers a forced turn. A forced turn is one which a course-following priority compels you to take. For example, if the instructions have put you *onto* Main Street, then you follow Main Street until an instruction specifically tells you to turn off or until you arrive at a checkpoint. Main Street may veer, jog, even make a 90-degree turn—the 90 would be a forced turn. Now the trap. Suppose you come to an intersection for which there is no instruction. The first thought is to continue straight ahead, but the protected-road priority makes you check out the three or more other available points of the intersection. If the two roads at 90 degrees to you have stop signs, and the one ahead does not, you continue straight. If the road to the right has a yield sign, and the road straight ahead has a stop sign, but the road to the left has no stop or yield sign, you will turn left.

Course-following priorities are real mind-benders in big league rallying and the SCCA Nationals play them big. Probably the best example of the priority game was done by award-winning rallymaster Wayne Zitkus in the 1971 Andiamo National Rally General Instructions. Zitkus is an expert rallymaster and competitor, and he is Chairman of the SCCA National Rally Board. We will quote directly from his text and diagrams, because we know we cannot improve on his work.

"At all intersections of public roads, apply the following rules in order of priority given to remain on course unless execution of a route instruction entails the contrary:
1. Stay on the prescribed route as determined by:
   a) Put on road by name or number*
   b) Black-on-yellow curve arrow signs*
   c) Protection through stop or yield signs*
   d) Center lines on pavement*
2. If you cannot go through an intersection by using 1-a, -b, -c, or -d, go straight*, or as nearly straight as possible through the intersection.
   * Defined in National Rally Regulations...."

A very important part of the technique of championship rallying is the method of recovery from an off-course excursion. Sooner or later even the best competitors go off the route. At the point where you realize you are wrong, make a note of the time and mileage and turn around. Record the time and mileage back to the point where you left the course. Note the mileage when you rejoin the course, double that figure, and then deduct it from your log. You now have true miles again, and it should be fairly accurate. Now for speed. Chances are you traveled down your off-course excursion on the average, but you probably made the return trip at flank speed. In this case you must take the watch time for the return trip and note it on scratch paper. Then calculate the time for a one-way trip on the off-course mileage on the average speed. Add these two times together, and that is the total lost time you need to make back. Odometers that subtract can be a big help in getting the odo right on when you rejoin the course, but you must note the mileage before you set the odometer to subtract, otherwise you won't have the mileage figure you need to calculate the time lost on the trip out at average speed.

Some computers are completely capable of handling the entire off-course recovery problem for you as long as you rejoin the course at the exact point you left it. The dandy little black box we run has one toggle switch that says merely "lost." When we go off course, we note the numbers reading on mileage and time on our log, just for safety's sake, push the "lost" button and the computer subtracts the miles and calculates the down time as it goes along. Upon reaching the point of our initial mistake, we flip the "lost" switch to off, and continue. True mileage and down time show clearly on the face of the counter.

Course recovery gets tricky, and if you take a short cut to get back on course it also calls for a good bit of educated guessing and ball park compensating. A background in SOP rallying is extremely handy in this case. We know folks both in SOP and full computer class who can recover from a long drive to nowhere, find the course downstream someplace, guesstimate their lost time and mileage from maps and the route instructions, and show up at the next checkpoint, if not on time, at least in the same minute.

The trend today in time-speed-distance rallying is toward the trap rally, for it equalizes the chances of an overall win throughout the classes far more than a timing contest. Undoubtedly the most monumental trap rally we know of is an SCCA National of great reputation: The Heart of Dixie rally, which is organized by the Tennessee Valley Region around Huntsville, Alabama. This group not only uses multiple traps in one instruction, but pioneered the "variable main road rule" in the championship series. The "variable main road rule" is as variable as the name implies, and is a further extension of route-following priorities. It is so involved one couldn't move from the starting point without reading the GIs, and there is at least one trap on each numbered instruction. The Heart of Dixie is a fine example of a trap rally. The 1973 rally had traps based on everything from the variable main road rule to multiple use of the same sign.

The competitive rallyist will eventually find himself filing a rally protest or claim. Since rallymasters and checkout crews are human, there will occasionally be a mistake on the route that no one but the competitors noticed. When people compete for points and an eventual championship, they tend to be serious about protesting a rally leg they think contained an error. Therefore most big events will have a claims committee made up of officials and one or two of the contestants.

The thinking rallymaster will include in his general instructions an allowance for delays and dead time. Normally one may ask for a time allowance for unusual situations such as waiting out the passage of trains at grade crossings, being delayed by military convoys, funeral processions, or accidents (as long as they do not involve the rally car), having the roads closed by police, and meeting herds of cattle and sheep. The procedure for requesting a time allowance is spelled out in the rally general instructions, and usually a claim form is included. Usually the claim must be substantiated by a witness, such as another rally car, but it all depends on the situation. You won't get a time allowance for changing a flat tire on your own car or having a conversation about legal speeds with the law, but you will receive the time if you are detained by a highway safety check. In any case, you calculate your down time and ask for an allowance in whole minutes, or at best half minutes. Hand the claim slip to the checkpoint worker at the next control.

Protests about timing or course-following are quite another thing. Sometimes a leg is thrown from a rally without a formal protest from competitors. For instance, and it is not uncommon, there is the missing sign syndrome. It can occur when a homemade sign or arrow has to be used to mark the route. Local people watch the first half of the rally go by, then either remove the sign or point it in a different direction, and there goes the rest of the field on a nonexistent course. And that leg of the rally would have to be thrown out.

The same problem can arise with a bona fide highway sign or billboard. A road may bear the name Highway 14 for 20 years, and the steel signpost be imbeded in the concrete for the same length of time. But on the day before the rally, state highway workers will erect a new sign that says Interstate 5 or they'll move the Hwy 14 sign to another location. This sort of thing does happen with an amazing frequency. The leg would have to be remeasured and true time recalculated or the leg would have to be thrown from scoring. There are hundreds of other problems that do call for a legitimate protest on the course.

The other side of the protest scheme is on timing. It is not impossible to receive a poor call or a misread watch on the best of controls on the top rally of the year. Anyone can read a watch wrong under stress, and if you have accurate on-board records of your time, you are qualified to post a timing protest. Normally you would ask the checkpoint workers to check the time call on the spot, and if they stick to their original call, you must then ask for extra dead time in the control, usually granted, and fill out a protest on the spot and file it with the checkpoint captain. If you are correct, and other cars around you can help back up your claim, you will usually get the time on your score that you requested.

One other major form of protest is the protest on the results themselves. At the rally's end you will be given the true times, and you will know your own leg times from your log. If all scoring is done on an in-the-car card, you should make a copy of your card before you turn it in or at least be sure it all matches your log. It can happen, especially on a rally with a large entry, that your card with its low or winning score gets lost in the shuffle or is refigured with some extra error tucked into a leg. When the scores are posted and your posted score doesn't match what your log says, you can ask for a recount; if you don't keep your own records for this type of problem, you may see cars with a higher score than yours in your class receive a trophy while you go empty-handed. On scoring where the individual time slips are used and all totals are figured by the scoring committee, you must also keep your own records. You must check your posted score against your log, and be sure it all matches.

While there are plenty of situations that make for a legitimate protest from the contestant ranks, there is also the type of rallyist who is a "protest artist." He can very often protest himself from fourth to first on minute technicalities. People like this are seldom popular with fellow contestants, and we know of one team who gained such a reputation for protesting themselves into a good finishing position on incredible items of detail that their entry was refused on two recent SCCA national rallies, and the organizers had the full support of the SCCA national headquarters in the action. Generally though, the era of the protest artist passed from SCCA national competition with the 1960s and the heavily sponsored factory teams. Today even the sponsored entries make every effort to win on the road instead of at the claims committee meeting.

There is no generalization that can lead one through the trials and triumphs of navigational rallying. It is an individual experience, a learn-by-doing game, and as the tricks of the trade unfold it becomes more and more enjoyable. No two people, particularly the experts, can tell you exactly why they rally, or why they travel all over the country just to get to the location of a rally. Primarily it is an enjoyable sport in which one can invest as little or as much time and money as desired and still be relatively competitive each time around. It is a sport that married couples can pursue either as a team or paired off with other couples for variety. One group of experts we know draws straws for partners on several non-championship rallies a year, just for fun, and also to learn a bit from each team's particular techniques of rallying. The novice and the expert, and the hordes of rallyists in between all claim that they learn something new each time out. It is the sharpening of the skills, the constant expansion of knowledge of the game, that makes it so much fun. Getting one leg right on a difficult rally can be more fun than toting home a big trophy from a typical Sunday "handholder." That is essentially the attraction in the sport of navigational rallying.

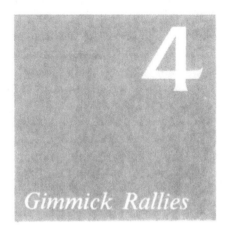

Gimmick Rallies

MANY RALLY ENTHUSIASTS like rallying but do not care for the time-speed-distance style of event. Some folks really have no desire to get that serious about rallying, and others prefer a different type of mind-bending run, so the gimmick rally is popular in many car club circles. The events are just what the name implies, and the style varies widely with no real standard format for a gimmick rally. Generally the gimmick requires nothing in the way of navigation equipment, and the team needs little in addition to the car and pencil and paper. There is no expensive equipment that will help the team, and gimmick rallies are quite popular for this reason, particularly with college car clubs and similar younger groups.

THE POKER RUN is the grand old man of gimmick rallies. The instructions call out route-following procedure, but ordinarily there is no tight time schedule. There will be an elapsed time for the entire run, and along the route either five or seven checkpoints. Instead of receiving a time at the control, each team draws a card from a standard deck of playing cards. At the

43

finish, the team with the best poker hand is the winner. Each control uses a marked deck of cards, so it is easy to see that each team has passed through all the controls to receive its full hand. If there are more than 52 cars, the control just shuffles together two decks of cards. The poker rally is an excellent event for a novice rallymaster and a family style outing. Variations on a poker run are myriad, and it can be combined with other types of rallies to increase the odds of winning.

THE MAP RALLY is another form of gimmick that can be quite a challenge. Each team is given a standard road map of the area, and instructed that only roads shown on that map are eligible rally roads. There are no route instructions in the familiar sense, and the rallyist will receive a written description of each checkpoint location. It might read something like "Ckpt 1 is 5.2 miles north of the intersection of State 78 and U.S. 60." The team must navigate to that intersection and then procede north on whatever road is available to find the control. Another form is to mark the map with checkpoint numbers and issue no written instructions at all. The team with the total odometer mileage closest to the shortest route to the checkpoint gets the low score for that leg, and the total lowest score is the winner. The checkpoint workers will record mileage at each control from the car's speedo, and usually have another gimmick in the route to insure passage of all cars in the proper route. A variation on the map rally is to have a time control at the checkpoint so that the rallyists must first find their way on the map and then TSD their way the last mile into the control. Both time and passage count toward the winning score. Many rallies have one leg or section of map navigating for variety within another form of event, and it can be quite a surprising challenge.

Variations on the map rally are plentiful, and one popular gimmick is the stick map which pops up in gimmick, Monte Carlo, and TSD events. The illustration shows how a stick map was used on an expert exercise style rally. Controls in the middle and at the end of the leg insure both time and proper passage: you have to approach the control from the proper direction. A stick map combined with a maze and an average speed has been used by top rallymasters in championship events.

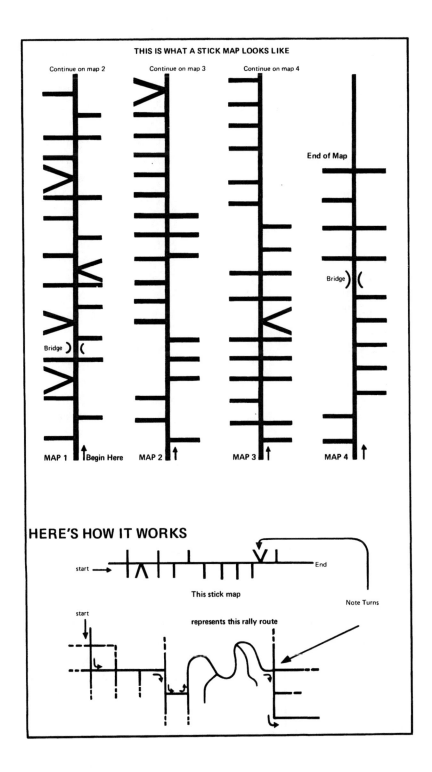

THIS IS WHAT A STICK MAP LOOKS LIKE

Continue on map 2   Continue on map 3   Continue on map 4

End of Map

Bridge) (

Bridge) (

MAP 1 ▌Begin Here   MAP 2 ▌↑   MAP 3 ▌↑   MAP 4 ▌↑

HERE'S HOW IT WORKS

start →   End

This stick map

Note Turns

start

represents this rally route

45

THE TREASURE HUNT or scavenger hunt is another common gimmick rally. The rally route is defined by instructions, and there are usually some on-course checkpoints, but these are often passage controls. There is a maximum time between controls, or a total time allowance, but the driving chores should be easy. The items to be found and presented at the finish may be quite tricky, and the team that finds the greatest number of items is the winner, and the least amount of elapsed time is used for a tie-breaker. There is no limit to the variety of the treasures one hunts, and the type and scope of items depend on the imagination of the rallymaster. A favorite trick is requiring something that is readily available in stores, but on a day when the stores are closed. Another popular gimmick is to send everyone hunting for a year-old copy of a magazine like *Road & Track*. About the only things you might eliminate from the treasure hunt are things which are too large to fit in the average rally car.

THE PHOTO RALLY is another gimmick and it indicates that the rallymaster has another hobby that involves photography. In the photo rally, all course-following directions are keyed by photographs. Sometimes even the checkpoints are identified by photos, and you must use a map to find them. For example, a roadside cafe, well known in the area, may be photographed from an angle that disguises its identity; hidden in the background of the picture will be a highway sign that will identify the general area. These rallies too are scored on a generous elapsed time basis, with the shortest mileage being the factor that determines the winner.

THE KITCHEN TABLE or armchair rally is a form of map rally that is quite literally run in your own home. The most famous of all such rallies is the St. Valentine's Day Massacre, a mail order event dreamed up some years ago by the Concours Plaines Rallye Team based in Chicago. For less than ten dollars entry fee you are provided with a new Rand McNally Road Atlas, full instructions, jacket patches, and souvenirs, all mailed on February 14. The route is thousands of miles long, and the instructions are cunningly designed to be full of traps. The Massacre provides snow-bound rallyists with a full month of mind-bending problems; all entries' answers must be postmarked back to Chicago by March 15. The results are done on a

46

computer, and prizes and trophies go to the top ten percent in two classes, Master and Non-master. There may be other mail-order rallies, but the St. Valentine's Day Massacre, which draws over 1500 entrants every year, is undoubtedly the best known.

THE QUESTION-AND-ANSWER GAME is probably the most standard gimmick rally of all. The route instructions contain questions about signs and landmarks along the way. The questions are worded in an obscure manner, and they can be predicated on any subject, so the rally becomes a game of solving riddles and puzzles. In some areas the Q & A style of gimmick rally has been refined to a fine art, and there are groups of car clubs which organize a championship series of gimmick rallies each year. The gimmick rally council in Southern California, for instance, puts on some extremely challenging course-finding rallies. Their route instructions and general instructions are quite similar to those of any top TSD trap-type rally.

GENERAL INSTRUCTIONS
FOR A QUESTION-AND-ANSWER GAME

At all times please observe the California maximum speed limit of 55 mph for trucks.

There is a California law which states that vehicles must pull off the road at the first possible point to let vehicles pass if they are impeding the progress of 5 or more vehicles.

When traveling, especially on freeways, watch your rear view mirrors at all times.

ROUTE INSTRUCTIONS

inst. no.		official mileage
1.	Begin rally at START. The STARTER will tell you when to go. (Navigator note odometer reading).	0.00
2.	You have 20.00 minutes to reach Instruction No. 13, a distance of 12.00 miles from the START.	
3.	Turn LEFT at the STOP SIGN.	0.26
4.	Turn RIGHT at the SIGNAL.	0.28

QUESTION 1: *How many signs reading "SCENIC ROUTE" do you see between Instruction No. 4 and No. 8?*

5. Continue straight towards SPORTS ARENA BLVD.   0.50

6. Follow signs towards SEA WORLD DRIVE.   0.93

7. Continue straight. Do not go towards INGRAHAM   1.26
ST or W MISSION BAY DRIVE.

8. Follow signs toward LOS ANGELES onto INTER-   3.00
STATE 5.

QUESTION 2:   *How many signs reading "DO NOT
PASS" do you see between Instruction
No. 8 and No. 9?*

9. Turn RIGHT onto LA JOLLA VILLAGE DR   10.37
OFF-RAMP.

10. Bear RIGHT at the end of the OFF-RAMP.   10.61

11. Turn LEFT at the STOP SIGN.   11.47

12. Turn RIGHT at the STOP SIGN (Eastgate).   11.81

13. At the sign reading "CONTROL DATA CORPORA-   12.00
TION," switch drivers and then leave this point
exactly 20.00 minutes after your START time and
maintain an average speed of 48 mph.

QUESTION 3:   *How many YELLOW FIRE HYDRANTS
are on the RIGHT-HAND SIDE OF THE
ROAD ON WHICH YOU ARE TRAVEL-
ING between Instruction No. 13 and No.
14?*

14. Turn RIGHT after a sign reading "FRAZEE   14.68
PAINTS" and maintain an average speed of 15
mph. (Road is named MILCH).

15. Turn LEFT at CONSOLIDATED.   14.70

16. ENTER CHECKPOINT. Do not stop until you   14.89
reach the timing personnel.

17. Execute a U-TURN at the END OF THE ROAD.

18. Begin LEG 2 of the RALLY at the second   0.00
RAILROAD CROSSING. Leave this point at your
assigned out-time and maintain an average speed of
15 mph. (Navigator note odometer reading).

19. Turn RIGHT at MILCH. (Give right-of-way to the   0.03
vehicles entering the checkpoint area).

THE *GIMMICK* TRAP RALLY also uses off-course controls to add penalty points, and they have questions about sights that can only be seen on the right course. The questions add a little spice—and points—just as the time controls would do on a TSD event. College car clubs are especially fond of this type of gimmick rally, and frequently the course-finding clues based on the general instructions are far more intricate than those in a championship TSD rally.

Beginner's rallies and rallies just for fun sometimes combine some gimmicks with a very simple time-speed-distance problem. The TSD section is done to teach the group what that kind of rallying is all about. The gimmick is based on sign reading, and the combination makes for easy tie-breakers if more than one team gets all of one section right. The example quoted here is from a TSD rally for rank beginners. There were no general instructions to confuse things, all conventions were included in the route instructions, and every route instruction was clued by mileage to make course-following as simple as possible. In order to separate the scores, the rallymaster included a question-and-answer sheet to be turned in with the route time card. To be sure of breaking a tie, there was a five-card poker feature too. Each team received two cards at the start, one at the first checkpoint, and two at the second checkpoint. They were given the draw-poker option of exchanging up to three cards at the finish. Scoring was done on the basis of percentages for the best time, the best score on the questions, and the best poker hand, with the highest percentage combination of all three winning the rally.

Any outing, whether it's a tour to a picnic or a day at the beach, can be enlivened by adding a gimmick rally to the drive. All that is really needed is a crew for the start and a crew for the finish; the rally can be one leg with questions. Gimmick rallies provide great varieties of adventure for the organizer and low pressure sport for the participants—just one more method of recreation involving the automobile.

Rallyese

LIKE ANY SPORT, rallying does have its own language. The first-time rally contestant may be totally bewildered by some of the terms he hears, and many of the terms may be local custom (more so than most national sports). The Sports Car Club of America loosely defines the abbreviations and conventions used on its championship rallies, but they leave the door open for local options, so long as the local terms are thoroughly illustrated in the general instructions.

The beginning competitor may want to quit before he starts when he hears someone say "We took a 5 when we bought the RIP 'Loitering' before the forced turn at T." Translation: the team followed an instruction that told them to change their average speed at a sign that read in part "Loitering," but they should have waited until they reached a second such sign to make the speed change, and their error cost them five hundredths of a minute.

Club rallies have their own language, of course, and the language is typical of the geographical area, normally. However, there are a good many terms that are in common use all over the country, so let's list them. This list we give here is an example of those terms which are common to navigational rallying. It is by no means intended to serve as a guide to any particular rally and its terms. (For that information, look in the general instructions.)

We must confess to lifting the list from a Southern California rally club's Friday night "learner" rally. The group, the Santa Monica Sports Car Club, has been in the rally business for over twenty years. These definitions and abbreviations are taken from their rally general instructions.

R—Turn right.

L—Turn left.

C—Continue.

OPP—Opportunity: a paved, public, through road onto which you may legally turn in the direction indicated.

FLR—Follow the lined road. A lined road is a road with a single or double center line. A lined road is considered continuous even though the line may be broken for short distances, especially at intersections.

CAST—Change average speed to or continue average speed of.

WOF—Whichever occurs first. Execute the part of an instruction that occurs first along the route, then cancel the other part(s).

SOL—Sign(s) on left.

SA—Sign(s) anywhere.

SIGNAL—The joining of two or more eligible rally roads at which your travel is intended to be controlled by at least one standard red-amber-green traffic signal, working or not.

STOP—A conventional octagonal stop sign intended to control your travel.

LANDMARK—An object along the course. Such object will be indicated in the route instructions by capital letters without quotation marks.

NOTE—A supplemental unnumbered instruction among the numbered instructions. It may be executed any time after execution of the preceding numbered instruction. It may be executed only once unless the NOTE states otherwise. It is not necessarily executed before the next instruction. A NOTE is considered cancelled when you enter the first checkpoint after the introduction of the NOTE, or by any instruction that so states. If a NOTE and a numbered instruction appear to conflict, the numbered instruction takes precedence, but does not cancel the NOTE.

These definitions cover only what would be applicable to that particular Santa Monica club rally, and they could be varied the next week on an event sponsored and conducted by the same club. Here are a few more terms in common use today:

FOLLOW usually means the same as continue. The street identified in the instruction by name or number should be followed even though it turns away from the most straightforward direction. Normally an instruction to CONTINUE or FOLLOW also means that you must find an identifying sign prior to executing the next numbered instruction.

PICK UP is used as: PICK UP HWY 71. It often occurs when the street on which the rally is traveling undergoes a name change. Usually the direction of travel does not change.

RIP—Reading in part. Refers to a sign or landmark where only part of the reading matter is quoted in the instruction. For example "Sierra" could appear on a sign reading "Sierra Hwy" or "Sierra Pines," and so on. Use of RIP is fading from popularity, and signs are explained in the generals these days as reading in part or whole.

GIs—General instructions, also known as generals. These pages are the basis on which the rally is written and scored. A club will use a set of general instructions for an entire season, and for each rally perhaps add a sheet of additional instructions for that event only.

The Sports Car Club of America's Rally Regulations include a glossary of commonly used route instruction terms. SCCA goes into greater detail than the local clubs on what constitutes a turn, and explains terms that are often covered in general instructions. The SCCA glossary is used as an advisory regulation by SCCA regions; the definitions given in the SCCA Rally Regulations are in effect on any sanctioned SCCA rally unless otherwise specified in the rally's general instructions. Anyone involved in SCCA rally competition needs the rally regs on board in the rally car.

The SCCA glossary includes these terms:

ACUTE—A turn of substantially more than 90 degrees at an intersection where there exists more than one opportunity to turn in the direction indicated.

AT—"Even with" for speed changes, mileages, etc.; "in the vicinity of" for turn instructions, etc.

BEAR—A turn of substantially less than 90 degrees at an intersection where there exists more than one opportunity to turn in the direction indicated.

BEFORE—Any navigational aid identified by the use of the word "before" shall be visible from the execution point of the instruction.

BLINKER—A warning signal, as at a highway or railway intersection, consisting of a light or lights, usually red or yellow, operating in an alternating sequence of off and on. A blinker (traffic light) may or may not be operating.

CROSS—To go straight across. To cross a divided highway is to cross both halves of it.

CROSSROAD—An intersection at which two public roads cross each other at approximately right angles.

FREE ZONE—A part of the timed rally route in which there are no timing controls.

GAIN—To make up a specified time during passage of a specified distance. The gain time is subtracted from the time required at the given average speed to traverse the specified distance. The specified distance in which a gain is operative is a free zone.

INTERSECTION—Any meeting or crossing of two or more public roads.

LEFT—A turn to the left of from 1 to 179 degrees.

54   LEG—The part of a rally route extending from one timing

control to the next, or from an assigned starting time to the next timing control.

MILEAGE APPROXIMATE / MILEAGE OFFICIAL—Both are distance measured from the start of a section to a point along the rally route. Mileage approximate is measured to within 0.1 mile; mileage official is measured to within 0.01 mile.

PAUSE—To delay a specified time at a named point or during passage of a specified distance. The pause time is added to the time required at the given average to traverse the specified distance. The specified distance in which a pause is operative is a free zone. (Pause is often referred to as add time—ie: add 0.50 minute to true time at signal).

PAVED—A road having a hard surface such as concrete, brick, macadam, etc.

PICK UP—To go essentially straight onto a new road, route or surface.

RIGHT—A turn to the right of from 1 to 179 degrees.

SECTION—Any part of a rally route at the beginning of which the official mileage is zero and at the end of which the official mileage ends or reverts to zero.

STOP—An official octagonal stop sign at which the rally car is obliged to stop.

T—An intersection having the general shape of the letter T as approached from the base. It is not possible to go straight at a T.

TRAFFIC LIGHT—A signal light used on highways, especially at an intersection, to regulate movement of traffic. A traffic light may be set to operate as a blinker but is usually fixed, alternating red and green (and frequently including yellow as a transition between green and red) indicating stop and go (and caution).

TRANSIT ZONE—A part of a rally route in which there are no timing controls and in which no specific speed need be maintained. Either an exact time for passage, or a restart time from the end of the transit zone must be given. An approximate distance for the length of the transit zone is desirable.

TRIANGLE—An intersection of three roads in the general shape of a triangle or inverted delta, including within the intersection a generally untraveled grass, gravel, or other surface. It is not possible to go straight at a triangle. Only one instruction may be executed at a triangle. This definition applies whether or not the term "triangle" appears in the route instruction.

TURN—To make a change of course or direction at an intersection which would not have been made in the absence of the turn instruction. A turn shall not be executed by going straight.

UNPAVED—A road having a non-hard surface such as broken stone, gravel, dirt, etc.

Y—An intersection having the general shape of the letter Y as approached from the base. It is not possible to go straight at a Y.

Naturally there are local differences: in some places "Change average speed to" might be given as "Change speed to," but every phrase used will be explained completely in the rally's general instructions. The good rallymaster assumes that his competitors are starting with zero knowledge; he presents everything needed in the GIs.

Other items in common usage are conventions and priorities. Conventions are those rules which are known and accepted everywhere, but they too must be mentioned in the generals, *unless* it is an SCCA-sanctioned rally, where SCCA's rally regs apply. For example, the SCCA regs on conventions are expressed in this manner:

"The following conventions are so well known that they can be used without mention in the general instructions. If the rally committee wishes to eliminate or change any of these, it must cover the subjects in the event's general instructions.

Roads marked Private—Keep Out—No Outlet—Dead End—Not a through street—etc., do not exist.

Illegal entries and illegal turns do not exist.

Any road which clearly ends in a garage, plant entrance, or parking lot does not exist.

U-turns are never required without instruction.

Information given in parentheses in the route instruction shall be considered as helpful or informative but not essential for the completion of the route instruction.

Signs painted on the road surface will not be used.

When an instruction identifies a route by number, it will not necessarily specify State, County, U.S. or Interstate.

Whenever route instructions are referenced to mileage (or to equivalent elapsed time), correct execution of the instructions shall not require determination of the mileage [more precisely then to within .1 mile.]"

We have found that most of these conventions are in use all over the country, but they are usually spelled out in the rally GIs as well. A good organizer leaves nothing to chance, and although he may use the SCCA rally regs, he goes over the same ground in his GIs. We have also found that signs on buildings, mailboxes, paddlemarkers, and the like are generally out of favor for rally instructions these days.

Route-following priorities are quite another thing: in the central part of the United States they are used on championship rallies. Again we quote from SCCA's national rally rule book, where priorities are also called "the main-road rule."

"It shall be considered sufficient to list in the General Instructions one or more of the following approved 'Route Following Priorities' by their title line only. When more than one is used, they must be listed in order of priority...."

"PUT ON A ROAD BY NAME OR NUMBER
"When directed onto a named, numbered or lettered road by use of the terms on, onto, or pickup, and the name, number or letter of the road in a route instruction, stay on that road until a subsequent course-following instruction can be executed. If an unmarked intersection is encountered or the route designation ends, continue on course as if instructed onto a road without indication of name, number or letter. If the name, number, or letter road is reincountered prior to executing the next

course-following instruction, stay on the road as described in this paragraph.

"BLACK-ON-YELLOW CURVE ARROWS

"Stay on the prescribed rally route as determined by official highway black-on-yellow curve arrow signs and black-on-yellow directional arrows. These signs are to be used with the same intent as that of the erecting agency.

"CENTER LINES ON PAVEMENT

"Stay on the prescribed rally route as determined by following center lines. Center lines are usually painted white or yellow and are continuous or dashed. These lines are to be used with the same intent as that of the establishing authority.

"PROTECTION BY STOP OR YIELD SIGNS

"Stay on the main road as determined by Stop and Yield signs causing traffic on lesser roads to give right of way to the main road. The rally route leaves the intersection by the road that does not have a Stop or Yield sign on the road if it is the only such road. The existence of a Stop or Yield sign on the road on which you enter the intersection is immaterial.

"STRAIGHT AS POSSIBLE

"It is to be understood that this priority would take contestants on the road that appears to go straight or as nearly straight as possible through the intersection. This priority will take the contestant through 'slant' tees, unequal wyes, and multiple intersections. The determination of which road is straight or nearly straight is made at the intersection in question and roads are judged on their merits as they enter the intersection, not how they look as you approach the intersection."

What this really means is that if the priorities are listed in the general instructions in the above order, the top preference would be the "onto" a road by name or number and that would be what you would follow in the absence of a numbered instruction at an intersection. If you were not working on a road by name or number, the next precedence for the same problem would be the curve arrows, which you would follow, and so on down the list. Frequently, traps are based on these priorities, and one or more can be used in any order listed in the generals.

At this point, the reader can easily see that TSD rallying can involve word games as well as mathematics and driving skill. The casual reading of both the Santa Monica and SCCA rules will seemingly produce the same results on the road. But there are subtle differences that could put one off-course, depending on the rally and which club was the organizer. The championship rallies, with top caliber people in the entry, must play the words as well as every other facet of the sport in order to separate the most talented of the top rallyists on score.

We must say again that the terms we have defined here do not apply to any particular rally, but they are examples of what you will encounter on any TSD event from a Friday-nighter to the National Championship. None of it is as frightening as it looks on paper. Most of the terms like OPPs and PICKUPs become familiar to the novice team before the first event is over. A great deal of it falls easily into place as you go down the route.

Suppose you are working on a NOTE "Right at each T," and the numbered instruction is "Right first OPP." To further complicate the problem, the previous numbered instruction would have put you "onto Main St." You are now traveling on Main Street, and the street ends in what appears to be a T. Remembering that "onto" is the top priority, you must first be sure that neither street on the top of the T is labeled Main. If it were you would automatically follow it without using any instruction. OK it isn't Main, so you can't continue on Main. You can then execute the unnumbered NOTE of "Right at each T" or you can use the numbered instruction "Right first OPP." Now, either usage would make you turn right, but the important thing is to turn right for the proper reason, so that you're unraveling the rallymaster's cunning little game as you go along. That is where the priority comes into play. Suppose the GIs list NOTES as taking preference over numbered instructions; you would turn right at the T on the NOTE, and still keep looking for the "Right first OPP" before going on to the next numbered instruction. On the other hand, if the GIs list numbered instructions as taking precedence over NOTES, you would turn right on the "Right first OPP," and move on to the next numbered instruction for your next action point. It really works much easier on the road than it does on paper, and that particular right turn is what is called a "trap." If you turn right for the proper reason, you stay on the course. If you use the wrong reason for the turn, the next instruction you execute would put you into an off-course loop or control. Traps are explained further in other chapters; this is merely an example of how they apply.

Rallyese becomes self-explanatory as one gets well into TSD rallying, but since the SCCA national rally regs allow for a good many local options in usage and terminology, both the long-time expert and the novice alike must check the general instructions of each rally to see how these rally terms will be used.

Average Speeds

AVERAGE SPEED CALCULATION is the catalyst that produces the competition of a time-speed-distance rally. Once past the pure SOP novice stage, the team must begin some method of determining how close they are to the stated average speed at all times. The SOP pencil-paper-and-stop-watch system has been covered in the beginner section, but the vast majority of rally people want to move forward from that class sooner or later. To do so you will need at least one odometer and one accurate watch, and those items are covered elsewhere. Here we will go into the considerable variety of methods of using the time and distance figures of the odo and watch to arrive at your actual position in average speed.

Average speed is really easy to figure. For example, it takes two minutes to cover a mile at 30 mph, 1 minute at 60 mph, and so on. Conversely at 30 mph you would cover one tenth of a mile in 12 seconds, half a mile in one minute, and so forth. That works keen, but few rally speeds will be quoted in such easy numbers.

Today the trend in average speeds is toward the whole number, but there are still plenty of rallies with averages of say

The Stevens is the best known of all slide rules designed for rally work. It is the ideal first tool for the novice, and it can be helpful in Class B or as a backup for the expert.

21.6 mph or worse 24.66 mph. This practice came about to catch the computer and cumulative calculator group, but in recent years traps have replaced the decimal speeds for that purpose, and most averages are quoted in whole numbers. Navigational aids that will calculate average speeds for you include rally tables, slide rules, circular slide rules, and the various derivations of the circular slide rule designed just for rallying. The next step, and one that puts you into the top class in nav work, is the use of a Curta or similar cumulative calculator, or the use of a computer. Computers are little black boxes installed in the car and driven by the speedo cable. They range from the relatively simple Halda Speed Pilot to the complete on-board digital computer that might call for an experienced programmer. We will explore the basics of rally navigation using each system of calculating average speed.

The base equation for figuring average speed is: Distance (miles) = Rate (mph) x Time (minutes). Other versions of that equation are: $R = D \div T$ and $T = D \div R$. In the car you will always have one factor unknown, and one of these equations will do the job. The three equations, using hours and minutes and seconds, look like this:

DISTANCE

$$\text{miles} = \text{mph x hours}$$

$$= \frac{\text{mph x minutes}}{60}$$

$$= \frac{\text{mph x seconds}}{3600}$$

RATE

$$\text{mph} = \frac{\text{miles}}{\text{hours}}$$

$$= \frac{\text{miles x 60}}{\text{minutes}}$$

$$= \frac{\text{miles x 3600}}{\text{seconds}}$$

TIME

$$\text{hours} = \frac{\text{miles}}{\text{mph}}$$

$$\text{minutes} = \frac{\text{miles x 60}}{\text{mph}}$$

$$\text{seconds} = \frac{\text{miles x 3600}}{\text{mph}}$$

You are assigned the average speed in mph, so that is always or nearly always a solid fact. The time comes from your watch and the mileage from the car odometer, so the most common equation is: Time = miles divided by the average speed.

Obviously this involves a good deal of mathematics on the fly. It is simple arithmetic, and it can be done with a pencil and paper, but it is far more simple to use some of the navigational aids available on the market for calculating these problems. You will have enough other work to do on the rally. Beyond pure SOP work, the unequipped rallyist should use some form of rally tables, and there are many commercially available. Most well known perhaps, and quite complete, is *Larry Reid's Rally Tables,* published by Sports Car Press. This book contains tables that cover speeds from 12 mph to 60 mph in 0.1 mph increments and gives the time in minutes and seconds it takes to drive from one to 40 miles at any speed within this range. Of course if you travel farther than 40 miles at a given average speed, highly unlikely, you need only double the numbers. The tables can provide true elapsed time for any even mile at a glance, and miles and fractions of a mile by adding two or three figures taken from the tables. The book also includes speed correction factors, sets of decimal equivalents and information on how to use them. To our knowledge, this is the only book of tables geared to seconds, where the beginning rallyist will be working on a wrist watch. There are plenty of other tables on the market: Floyd's Factors, Navig-Aider Cards, Stinson's Factors, Rally Tally, Autopacer, and more. These are geared to the decimal minute, by far the most common system of rally scoring.

Using factor tables for rally navigation is the least expensive method of playing the game. However, one must be sure that the tables will work with corrected average speeds. It is a rare occasion when your odometer will match the rallymaster's measurement exactly, so you will use an odometer correction factor gained by dividing your mileage reading by the official mileage reading at the odo check. You can correct your own average speeds by multiplying each quoted average by your odo correction factor, and then turn to the proper table, but this costs a bunch of time. You can save that time by using a set of tables for corrected average speeds, available from Rally Tally or Norman Cone's Corrected Minutes-Per-Mile Factors. The choice and number of factor cards is an area where the novice team should observe carefully what is in common use around them, and also borrow a set of cards, if possible, before making a purchase.

The only factor card system we have ever used personally is the Autopacer. The system consists of three parts: the factor finder, the factor cards, and the speed cards. The factor finder, a logarithm table, is used to determine the odometer correction factor. All one does is subtract the two mileages at the odo check and look up the factor in the tables. Next you pull out the factor card for that correction factor and it shows corrected mileages from 1 to 100, so you can correct all official and speed change mileages to match the car's odometer reading. The speed cards contain a time for each tenth of a mile from 0.1 to 1 mile. It can get busy in the car, if speed changes occur in less than a mile. In some areas the use of this system will push the team out of SOP class, but it does make the math a good deal more simple.

Moving up from pure factor card running, the next step is use of a slide rule. There are several designed just for rally work, and we still have a small Blackwell acquired back in 1957. If you are buying, the Stevens and the Taylor are available at most rally outlets and are large enough to be read easily on the fly or at night. They will handle the odometer correction factor too.

The Stevens Rally Indicator is doubtless the best known of all such devices, so much so that Stevens has become a generic term for rally-style circular slide rules. The Stevens slide rules come in two sizes, six inch or nine inch diameter scale. The larger retails for under $15. We recommend the larger one because it is easier to read in a moving car.

The Stevens is a single laminated-plastic dial with three aluminum arms (marked T, M, and E) pivoted from its center. There is one highly legible outside scale printed under a transparent plastic surface. The long arm, marked T, is used to rotate all three arms which are locked together in rally use by knurled thumb screws. T indicates time in minutes. M can be rotated in relation to T to indicate miles. E indicates odometer correction; it also rotates with M. After you compute your odo correction factor, set up the slide rule as follows: Set the M pointer on official mileage and hold it there. Set the E pointer on your odo figure. Lock E and M together, and don't unlock them for the rest of the rally. The M pointer is used for all instruction mileage, and the E pointer will read the same as your odometer. The T pointer reads time.

For example, to set in the average speed of 34 mph after the odo check, you place the T arm on 60, the M arm on 34, and tighten the the thumb screw. To take a time reading, set the E arm on your odo mileage reading and read the corresponding time in minutes on the T arm. To take a mileage reading, set the T arm on elapsed time in minutes from the last speed change

65

and read corresponding mileage on the E arm. You must, of course, reset the Stevens for each new average speed at the mileage where the action occurs, taking care not to disturb the odo correction thumb screw set.

The Taylor calculator uses two identical eight-inch scales. The outer reads in minutes, the inner in miles and mph, and it operates on much the same principle as a normal slide rule. On the Taylor you can carry your odometer correction factor by figuring a percentage and offsetting the scale to read corrected time. Another, similar, device is the Auto Rally Monitor; it has three scales, one of which carries the odo correction factor. Anyone skilled in the use of a standard or circular slide rule can use either of these slide rules for rally calculations. However, we feel that the novice navigator has enough problems without introducing the mysteries of slide rule operation.

It has been many years since we used a rally slide rule for navigation, and then we had a Stevens and are not familiar with the pros and cons of the others. We think that the Stevens is quite handy, and obviously accurate in application because many top national Class B rallyists use it. The Stevens is easy to read and adapts to off-course recovery problems as well. It is likely the Taylor and the others are equally handy in Class B. None of the slide rules are cumulative however, so they are legal in Class B. They do require precise logging of time and mileage at each speed change, though, if you wish total leg time to be accurate.

The use of any cumulative calculating device from an adding machine on up will move the team into the top navigational class: SCCA Class A. At one time the small mechanical adding machine was popular on rally trails, and today the mini electronic calculators are popping up in rally cars. These items are expensive, however, and for the most part they are not as useful for rally work as the ubiquitous Curta Calculator. The fabled Curta "pepper mill" was not designed with rally work in mind, but it is a miniature mechanical marvel—ideal for time-speed-distance work. The Curta is made in two sizes; the larger of the two measures about 2½ by 3 inches and weighs less than half a pound. It will do all manner of calculations, square roots—just about anything a desk calculator can manage. The Curta is completely mechanical (built in Lichtenstein—did you

The Curta calculator is by far the most favored of all hand-held devices in rally circles. The "pepper mill" is still for sale in this country, although it is no longer in production.

know that?), is simple to hand-crank, and has far more accuracy than the best slide rule. For rally navigation the Curta adds continually the minutes-per-mile factors, adds distance, displays time, and displays miles. The larger model will display both official mileage and odometer mileage.

To use the Curta for rallying you need a set of minutes-per-mile factor tables in decimal minutes, and ideally your watch should read in decimal minutes too; the car should be fitted with a pair of hundredths-counting odometers. The minutes-per-mile factor is the number of minutes required to travel a mile at a certain speed; it is found by dividing the speed into 60. For instance, it takes 2 minutes to travel a mile at 30 mph, so that factor is 2.000. It takes one and a third minutes to travel a mile at 45 mph, so that factor is 1.333. A set of factor tables or cards is quite necessary when navigating with a Curta, but you can make up your own using the Curta.

Curta operation for rallying is simple. Use the setting register to input the minutes-per-mile factor for the quoted average speed. Turn the crank, and the Curta will add time and mileage. The black dial on top will read in minutes; the white dial will read miles. The fineness of the result is determined by what carriage slot is used for input, and that is governed by what piece of the rally is being measured. Use carriage slot 1 for one

67

hundredth of a mile traveled, slot 2 for a tenth, slot 3 for 1 mile, slot 4 for 10 miles, and so on. The miles on the white dial should match the odometer; the minutes on the black dial should match the watch at the same moment.

You can run the Curta on elapsed time just like any other device, but it is simple to run the Curta on time of day. The rally is scored and maintained on time of day; the capability of doing all calculations in time of day is a major convenience of the Curta. To set up the Curta to do this, insert your time of day on the answering register. If you are scheduled to leave the odo check at 8:53, you put 53 on the Curta. (Disregard the hours since they will not add decimally.) Enter the 53 minutes on the answer register by putting the carriage on position 3, setting 53 on the slides (slot 8 and 7 on the small Curta, 11 and 10 on the large Curta), and turning the crank once. Then push the slides back to zero, and wipe out the "1" in the white dial by lifting the crank and subtracting once. The Curta now reads zero except for your out-time in time of day which you must match to your watch. Next you set the minutes-per-mile factor for the first average speed on the slides, matching the whole minute to the out-time slot. You are ready to give your driver a time check at every mile, tenth, or hundredth by comparing the time day reading on your watch with the time reading you crank out of the Curta.

Passing through an hour will make the Curta read more than 60 minutes. The number can get unhandy and it doesn't match the watch. So, in a spare moment you can subtract 60 from the time slot. Zero the slides and place 60 under the whole minutes. Then turn the crank once to subract, and zero the slides again. Add back the missing mile by turning the crank once in add position. When you put your average speed factor back on the slides, your watch and the Curta will once again match.

When you give time checks to the driver, remember that when the Curta and the watch match exactly you are on time. If the watch is ahead of the Curta, you are late by the difference, and if the Curta is ahead of the watch, you are early by the difference. At a speed change, the navigator must log the miles first, on his lap board log, when the driver says "Mark." Then he runs the Curta up to the miles of the speed change, and only then does he change the factor to the next speed. The

Curta is equal to any problem in rally navigation, and both sizes fit easily in the hand. The only thing better than the Curta for ease of operation in rally work is a computer attached to the car and driven by the speedometer.

We haven't dealt with an odometer correction on the Curta yet. There are two ways of handling that; the most simple is the use of corrected factor cards. In other words, when you find your odo correction factor, say 1.012, you go into the card file for the sheet with that correction, and put it on the clipboard or clip it to the dash. Throughout the rally you then insert the corrected factors for the average speed in the Curta, and Curta miles will match your odometer. If your factor is 1.012 your factor card would read 0.988 instead of 1.000 for a 60 mph average. If you need to add true miles, you can find out what your odo will read by multiplying the additional miles by the odo correction factor, and that will produce your odometer reading at the action point. If you have the large model Curta, you can run true factors and your white dial will read in official miles. You then set the odometer correction factor in the far side of the slides, so your odo reading will display on the register with some space between it and the calculated time.

The Curta is no longer made, but it is still available from many suppliers like Burns Industries. The advent of the mini electronic jobs that are also hand held has lessened the demand for the Curta by field engineers and other users. The Curta can often be acquired second hand, because many folks moving into a computer will sell their Curta. The used prices are generally a good deal less than new retail prices of $150 for the small Curta and $185 for the large one.

The final step is the on-board computer. A computer takes a good bit of the math work out of the rally sport. Most of the computers are digital computers. Although they perform the same tasks as the Curta, they do the work automatically, either by electrical impulse or by purely mechanical means; both types depend on a speedometer-driven cable. The Halda Speedpilot is the most reasonably priced of all computers; it is mechanical in operation and requires special speedo cables. It is of great value in Monte Carlo and performance-style rallies. The Halda requires only that you dial in the average speed and wind the clock. When the two hands on the time-of-day clock match, you

The Halda Speedpilot is the least expensive of the computers. It is of great value in performance rallies, but not accurate enough for TSD work.

are on time. Basically, this is what all computers do, but they vary greatly in how they are operated and in accuracy. Some computers are like electric Curtas, and they require that a minute-per-mile factor be fed in. Others need only the average speed and they take care of the rest. The prices for these devices run from under $100 for the Speedpilot to well over $1000 for a full computer complete with printout.

Benefits of the rally computer are many, but the primary one is that the TSD navigator can look at the course instead of **being** buried in paper work. The navigator can then help the driver spot signs and interpret the instructions in much the same manner as an SOP co-pilot, but in the meantime the computer is making sure that the team is right on time. That all reads out automatically on some dial of the computer. In recent months we have run several rallies operating a variety of the new generation of computers. We can honestly say we like it much better than slide-ruling or Curta-cranking for recreation. In operation the navigator merely figures the odo correction factor at the check, dials it into the proper slot, and then just checks the clock and turns the knobs for the average speed changes. All the while one counter or dial is reading "up/down" or late/early. You still keep a log, but it is no real hassle.

Computers make off-course recovery much less involved too,

and far less time consuming, but often the cost of the equipment is beyond the budget. Happily, the three or four rally computers available today can usually be purchased in stages. You can start with the basic unit and an impulse device, around $400, and go rallying. You will still need to use your old counters for odos, or rally with corrected average speeds, until you can afford the goodie that figures the odo correction for you. You may have to carry the pause or add-times manually too, because the add-time gadget costs a bit of money as well. Usually the home tinkerer has it all together in a giant box in a year or so.

We think computers are responsible for the sudden popularity of the trap rally. The sophisticated computer can handle any average speed change, so top rallymasters design traps in course-following to separate the pros. The individual computers are covered in the chapter on odometers, but if you want to be a consistent winner on TSD rallies in most parts of the country, the computer is your ultimate goal in equipment.

A neat and tidy installation of dual odometers in the glove box is augmented by the big Curta and clock on the clipboard. This car, with compass, is set for TSD or performance rallying.

Counting
the Miles

EXCEPT IN THE PURIST SOP class, the rally team learns to rely on the car odometer (mile counter) for one third of the time-speed-distance equation. Without consistently reliable odo numbers, it is impossible to figure average speeds. It is nice if the rally car comes equipped with a resettable trip odometer in the speedo. The trip odometer can be reset to zero, which makes it work well for the beginning rallyist. He doesn't need to buy a thing for mile-counting until he moves into a mechanical class. One can work with a total mileage counter, but it calls for a certain amount of subtractive math on the fly.

The odometer should be accurate, or close to accurate, in relation to the statute mile in order to provide a small, manageable number for the odo correction factor. If your car measures three percent or more error, common on a stock speedo, you can get it regeared at a speedometer shop. Changing tires will also increase or decrease your odo reading, because the distance measured on the odometer relates directly to the gearing in the instrument and the rolling radius of the tire.

73

The speedometer-odometer in the car is driven by a flexible cable rotating inside a flexible housing. The cable is driven by the car's transmission or, in the case of some rear-engined cars, by the hub of one front wheel. The speedometer head itself has a magnet, a field plate, and a speed cup, and the degree of its error is seldom linear. You will soon learn to compensate for an inaccurate speedometer and drive at the true average speed required. The odometer, however, is another matter.

The odometer is purely mechanical. The number wheels which can be seen through the instrument face are driven by a gear train which is driven by the speedometer cable. Every time the car's road wheels turn, the odometer advances. Most standard trip odometers register tenths of a mile, which is the legal limit in class B. If you plan to use your own trip odo for serious course measurement, be sure and check it out and have any giant error rectified by a change in gearing, making sure you have the rally tires fitted when the check and recalibration is done. With the odo calibrated close to the statute mile and a radial, non-expanding tire on the car, your mileage measurement will be in a comfortable ratio to the official rally miles.

Under Class B rules in SCCA and other associations, one tenths-counting odometer may be used whether or not it came with the car, and most rule books let you move it in front of the navigator. You can move the entire speedometer, but this is awkward and often illegal. You might move just the trip meter section or, better yet, buy an auxiliary odometer. You will need to buy a T-gear, which is a device that fits onto the speedometer head, accepts the speedometer cable, and drives an auxiliary cable to the new odometer. At this point you should buy your car a heavy duty speedometer cable from a speedometer shop, because the extra load from driving two instruments and an auxiliary cable may be more than the standard unit will take without whipping, breaking, or—worse—jamming the speedo head.

A good trip meter is not hard to find. Although most rally instruments measure to hundredths of a mile, there are counters available reading in tenths. You might find a bargain in an auto or motorcycle wrecking yard in the entire speedo from a vehicle that has a trip meter. The rally gear catalogs offer a choice of units ready to install on the dash. For instance, Competition

The Halda Twinmaster is the most widely used of all mechanical odometers, and the incidence of failure is quite low. Halda sells all over the world and parts are available anywhere.

Limited will supply a complete VDO motorcycle-type speedometer calibrated to whatever revolutions per mile your car's speedo cable turns. The speedometer has a resettable trip odo that will add or subtract, and it has an interior light. The cost complete with a cable to connect to your T-gear is about $50.

The rallyist who chooses Class A will find a huge array of odometers and computers readily available at sports car accessory and rally stores. Most companies can handle walk-in trade, and some, like Vilem B. Haan and MG Mitten, have elaborate showrooms. Still, most rally gear is sold by mail order. Big catalogs offering everything from driving gloves to computers are available from Haan, MG Mitten, Competition Limited, Rally International, Denco, Burns Industries, and many more. Check the glossary for these addresses.

The serious competitor will need at least one hundredths-counting odometer, for the simple reason that rallymasters measure the routes with hundredths-counting odometers. Although there are many styles, there are only two basic types of counters: electric and mechanical. In previous years Stevens Engineering and others built mechanical counters driven simply by gears and cables. Today the pure gear-driven counters have disappeared from the retail market with a couple of notable exceptions. The best known are the Halda counters, made in Sweden; they are the ultimate for European-style rallying. Halda's primary business is taxi meters, but they sell their rally counters in every country of the world where there are rallies. The basic unit is the Halda Tripmaster, a mechanical single

75

odometer that counts to 999.99 miles. It has a three-position switch for off/on, add, and subtract. The subtract feature is unusual for a mechanical odometer, and very handy. The Tripmaster resets to zero by a pull button and has a correction feature in a side-mounted knob that allows manual adjustment for fine corrections up or down. The Twinmaster is actually a pair of Tripmasters in a single chassis. Both models have lighted dials. These counters can be run separately, together, or in any combination of add and subtract. They are ideal where mileage is given at every instruction. The mechanical odometer is apt to be more sturdy for rough road running than the electrics, and the Halda is in great favor with performance rally addicts the world over.

The Halda units have another feature that brings them into a 99.6 percent of total accuracy. Halda makes the reduction gears for the instrument in over 30 combinations, so the Halda owner can buy sets of substitute gears. The gear change is quick and easy, and a chart is supplied so that you merely calculate your correction factor at the end of the odo leg, pop open the side of the Halda and install the proper gear. No tools are required, and extra gear sets cost less than $2 apiece. You can get the whole set of gears and a carrying case also. The Halda Tripmaster sells for about $75, the Twinmaster for $100. The Twinmaster is the better investment. All Halda instruments, including the Speed-pilot, require special Halda fittings on the cables and the T-gear; be sure to order the T-gear and cable for your car when you order the instruments.

Another readily available mechanical counter is the Aifab from Denmark. It is sold here in Gemini trip-counter sets, which consist of three counters, two registering in hundredths and reading to 99.99 miles and the third registering in tenths and reading to 999.9 miles. Each counter can be started, stopped, or reversed individually, and the drive gears can be changed to establish accuracy in a particular car. The counters are self-illuminated, and they all reset to zero with a push button. Aifab Gemini is also driven through a T from the car's speedo, or it can be driven from a gearbox on a non-driven wheel. The three-counter unit costs about $120.

These mechanical counters do their work in silence. This can be a mixed blessing: if the counter should quit, you would have

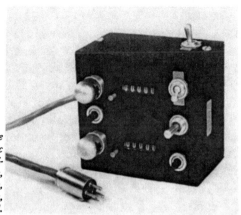

The most common of the over-the-counter electric odos is from Stevens Engineering. The counters, impulse unit, and cable, complete with instructions, can be ordered by mail.

to be looking at it to notice that is wasn't counting. Also, some navigators prefer to hear the constant click of the electric odos, and it aids their confidence. Many navigators will count down to the in-marker by the clicks rather than by visual observation. It all depends on what you prefer in nav systems.

There are numerous breeds of electric counters, and if you are truly ambitious you can build your own. For the sake of brevity, we will explore here only the Stevens electric counters. Stevens is the best-known brand in rally circles; Stevens equipment is available from a number of rally outlets and from the manufacturer, Stevens Engineering of Newport Beach, California. (By the way, Stevens has a neat little rally catalog also.) The Stevens single and dual electric counters and the speedometer impulse unit have been in constant development since first being marketed in 1957, and they are the most common of all the electric counters used in TSD work. The manufacturer claims 100 percent accuracy, not 99 percent plus fractions, and our personal experience with these counters backs up that claim completely. Stevens' basic counter is a five-digit, Veeder-Root, panel-mounted, electric unit (6 or 12 volts). It has a push-button reset, a counter light and light switch, an off/on toggle switch, plus a cord and plug to connect to the impulse unit. It is housed in a 4 by 2 by 3-3/4-inch aluminum cabinet complete with clipboard mounting holes and screws, all for around $40. The Stevens dual electric counter is just double the single—two sets of everything—neatly packaged in one cabinet. Either half can be used independent of the other, and there is a manual advance button (only on the dual units) to run up extra mileage or time.

Electric counters require an impulse unit which takes the place of the mechanical counter's T-drive. The flexible electric cable allows for easy mounting of the counters on a lap board. A mechanical cable has to run in a straight line from the speedo head to eliminate whip, but the electric cable can wander around the cockpit without a problem. The impulse unit built by Stevens consists of a housing with a speedometer-cable connector, a set of gears inside, and a threaded outlet for attachment to the car speedometer. The gears drive a tiny cam which trips a micro-switch—100 times per mile.

The Stevens impulse unit is justly famed for its reliability and accuracy. It can be ordered to fit any car imaginable, and for the real rally buff, a few more dollars spent will equip the impulse unit with an adjustable cam to allow a real zero on the micro switch and eliminate the last foot of mileage error. The basic impulse unit runs around $40. In fact, prices of the dual Stevens electrics and the impulse unit compare almost exactly with those of the Halda Twinmaster with cables and T-drive.

Those who rally in the dirt, snow, or in any circumstances where wheelspin is a problem, a non-driven-wheel odometer drive is a must. In most cars the speedometer cable is driven by the transmission. When the drive wheels spin, so does the odometer, whether the car is going anywhere or not. To remedy this, Competition Limited supplies an external odometer drive to fit either a standard wheel or a mag wheel. Other outlets provide a gear drive installed in a hubcap. Stevens supplies his electric impulse unit in a wheel cover. The external gearbox of a mechanical unit drives a speedometer cable which is routed over or through the fender and then under the hood to the odometers. These drives are geared precisely for the wheel and tire being used, and very rarely can be adapted easily to another size.

Any electric counter can be corrected at the source by use of an odometer correction gear box and set of extra gears. The gearbox and gears are available at most rally stores. After figuring your odometer correction, you merely install the proper gear in the odo correction gearbox next to the readouts, and your odos will record official miles for the rally.

The impulse unit is the heart of the electric odo system; impulse must be geared to the make of car. Adjustments for accuracy can be made by changing gears at the odo check.

Truly, there is a gadget to correct every possible flaw, and it can run into a good deal of money. The rallyist must observe carefully to see what style of equipment will best suit his needs, and be careful before plunging into the purchase of perhaps a hundred dollars worth of odometer equipment.

In the early years of rallying many people built their own electric odometers from counters available in war surplus outlets. With dual odometer setups available now for well under $100, it hardly seems worth the effort, but it is still possible and it could be fun for the devoted tinkerer. You will still need to purchase an impulse unit; be sure to order both the male and the female plug for the unit that fits your car. Installation of the impulse unit is simple. Like the mechanical T-gear, it screws onto the head of the speedometer. Then you merely connect one lead to a hot terminal and another to ground, and plug in the counter.

If you are building the counter either for fun or because of budget, or both, you will need to construct some sort of housing for it. The chassis can be made of aluminum, masonite, or even wood, and the shape will depend on whether you intend to mount the counter on the dash or on the lap board. You will need some 16-gauge wire, some terminal ends, a terminal strip with at least five posts, and a couple of toggle switches. Most of this can be found in a surplus store or radio store. The counter may also come from a surplus store or electrical supply house. Surplus counters may come from copying machines, turnstiles—any of the sundry modern counting devices—but be sure the one you find will be easy to read in the car.

Surplus electric counters will undoubtedly have to be rebuilt and rewired for rallying. If it is the Veeder-Root type of counter you have found, you should know how they work before trying to rebuild one. Inside the case will be a coil, possibly two, and when current is applied, a magnetic field attracts a striker plate which is linked to the digit wheels. Exercising the plate will cause the counter to register 00001 for each click. Normally you must replace the coils with 12 volt coils from an electrical supply house, and you will need two coils for each counter. Of course you could take the trouble to have the existing coils rewound. Now, with a screwdriver you can install the 12-volt coils. Be sure they go into the exact same spot because the upper surface of the coil determines the stroke of the striker blade.

The next step is to locate the counter on the dash or on your lap board, wherever it fits best. The wiring will be quite straightforward and should pose no problems.

There are two switches on a dual counter setup; toggle switches are very handy. One switch will select the left or right counter, and the second is used for adding counts or impulses to either counter. The switch is wired into the car through the power pin of the connector so that it will give a shot of current to the counter to which it is directed. This is used to add miles for correction. As you assemble the counters, be sure that all connections are secure and nothing touches anything else. Normally the microswitch has a life of over 100,000 miles and requires no interim maintenance. We must thank a long-time Southern California rallyist, Bob Henry, for the information on how to build a counter. As you can see, it isn't difficult to build a counter, but with the lack of suitable counters in surplus houses these days, it may be just as costly as buying the whole thing new.

There is another step beyond mere counters, and that is the digital or analog computer. We could easily fill the whole book on the development and the variety of rally computers on the road today. A good many of these computers are homebuilt one-off models that keep the electronic types busy at the work bench. We won't attempt to explore these units, but there are a few computers available that you merely buy and install with a minimum of fuss and bother.

The ancestor of all rally computers is the mechanically

Homebuilt computer resembles the Tommy Box. Bottom bank is for odo correction factor, top two are for the average speed working and the next average speed to be used. Counters will read time or mileage.

actuated Halda Speedpilot which is basically a pair of dials and a single, tenths counting odometer in a very compact package. One dial is a hand-wound 8-day clock with an extra hand or pointer; the other dial is an average speed indicator with a single pointer. In operation you zero the counter at the start of each leg, move the pointer to the quoted average speed on the left dial, and set the pointer hand on the clock to your out-time. When the minute hand on the clock and the clock pointer run together you are on time, and when they separate, you are early or late depending on the direction of the pointer lag from the minute hand. The Speedpilot is an analog device and cannot equal the accuracy of the electrically impulsed digital computers. But it is of great value on European style rallies, and it will keep to within about 20 seconds per hour in error. It allows one team member to rest while the other drives a long transit leg on performance rallies. The Speedpilot, like other Halda instruments, has a fine adjustment knob which allows you to dial in a correction at the end of the odo leg. It sells for around $100 and is by far the least expensive of all computer devices.

To our knowledge the "Tommy Box" was the first manufactured-for-resale electric rally computer built in this country. It was made by Captain H.E. Thomas, a retired naval officer and a long time devotee of rallying. He has a heavy background in

81

Odometer drive consists of the gearbox taped onto a non-driven wheel with a cable stretching off over the hood to the cockpit. Crude looking but it works.

electronics, and upon his retirement from the navy he began manufacturing his magic boxes for other rally folk. The first Tommy Box was truly an electric Curta with just one panel of knobs for setting in the minutes-per-mile factor. One had to rally with corrected factors. The original Tommy Box read out on two counters, one for time and the other for miles. Over the years Captain Tommy developed a two-bank system and then a three-bank system. The two-bank system lets the navigator preset the next speed change. The three-bank system allows him to insert the odo correction factor and use true minutes-per-mile factors. The three-bank system also has a dial like the Halda's, where the driver has merely to match the hands of the dial to his time-of-day watch and drive on time. The latest Mark XI Tommy Box has the two banks for minutes-per-mile factors and time and mile readouts; it hooks up to the odo-correction bank. The system works through a Stevens speedo impulse unit.

Similar to the Tommy Box is the Heuer/RoBo rally computer. It was developed by former SCCA National Champion Roger Bohl. Like the Tommy Box, the RoBo also has two banks for minutes-per-mile factors (so that the next average speed can be preset while the car is running on the current average) plus a bank for odo-correction factor. The RoBo has counters for off-course mileage and time, buttons for adding time or mileage, and a digital up/down counter for the driver: when it registers zero the car is on time. The RoBo is no longer made, but there are units still available from Heuer.

The second generation of rally computers is now upon us, and these are far more simple and compact than the early units. With the advent of integrated circuitry, the functions of the massive, early computers can now be contained in one small box. We have rallied behind one new computer called Rallecomp, built by RSR in Los Angeles; it is quite compact in size. One of the Rallecomp's most striking advantages is that it can be used in a basic form, with convenience accessories to be added as time and budget permit. The Rallecomp is a digital time-speed-distance computer designed just for American-style TSD work. It contains an accurate, crystal-controlled digital clock, time from which is compared internally to the computed time (a function of the distance traveled and the setting of the mph register). The difference between clock time and computed time is displayed on an internally lighted, easy-to-read counter. The driver attempts to keep the counter reading zero. Average speeds in mph can be programmed directly into the computer on two sets of thumbwheel switches: one set for running average and one for next average. The navigator no longer needs

Basic Rallecomp unit is small enough to fit any car. Integrated circuits allow this miniaturized computer to perform many functions and also control many optional bits of gadgetry.

to convert mph into minutes-per-mile. During the odo check the Rallecomp will function as a hundredths-reading electronic odometer. Using the basic instrument, the navigator figures the odo correction factor, and then from tables supplied with the computer he selects the corrected average speeds to be dialed into the computer. The basic Rallecomp sells for $400, and there are plenty of accessories available.

If the team wants mile counters, any electric counter can be programed through the Rallecomp, and computed-elapsed-time counters can also be attached. The odo-correction thumbwheel bank is available separately, and so is a remote up/down counter for the driver and a mile counter also for the driver's use. A time-of-day digital clock can be added, and there is almost no end to the gadgets for add-times, off-course recovery, and so forth.

The Zeron is a new and most interesting computer for 1973 (although we have never seen the unit in action). It is available in two models, the 330 and the 440. The 440 seems to perform just about every conceivable rally function, and includes large digit-light displays for time and mileage. The Zeron allows for direct average speed input on thumbwheel banks, has add-time and gain-time switches, a time-of-day clock, and a mile readout as well as computed time and off-course recovery functions. There is a remote up/down counter for the driver, and accessory gadgetry to cover any possible situation. Zeron is sold through Rally International and other equipment outlets.

A good commercially available computer is the Autonav, a solid state rally computer made by the Joslin Computer Company. It was one of the first to work directly in average speeds instead of minutes-per-mile factors. The Autonav comes complete with an impulse unit for around $500. The basic device has two average speed banks plus the odo-calibration thumbscrew bank, so you can rally without tables using the Autonav. There are no counters with the basic unit, but one of the add-ons is a well calibrated driver's guide, a circular one that reads zero when you are on time, for about $100. Joslin also offers a complete position-display box that has five counters reading in elapsed time, computed course time, odo miles, pauses and gains, and an auxiliary display of computed course time or miles. All this goes for about $250.

Readers must not take these quoted prices as gospel, for the year 1973 has seen rapid advances in the costs of electronic and imported components. The quotes are meant only to provide a ratio of value between these items, and not reflect the actual cost next year or even next month. You get what you pay for in the computer field, and prices vary only slightly from one make to another for the displays and services provided. Of them all the Rallecomp is the most reasonable initially that will get you down the road on a rally without extra stuff. That unit does allow the rallyist to add each additional function as he can afford it, which is probably the most practical method of moving into the computer set. On the average, the computer-equipped TSD team will have about $1000 in their equipment, including a crystal-controlled time-of-day digital clock. The components are generally trouble free, and seldom require any maintenance, which is quite a plus factor.

An example of the typical computer setup carried to the ultimate degree of gadgetry is one we rallied behind recently. The basic unit was the Rallecomp, but counters for all

A complete computer setup. Rallecomp at lower right gives average speeds and odo correction. Odos read every possible need, extra thumbwheels preset add-time, and counter at right is a quartz-crystal clock to augment the electric clock on the dash. Ultimate goodie is the printout, lower right.

conceivable purposes had been added. There was an odo correction factor bank, a large crystal digital clock, and an instant add-time feature that alone cost more than $100. The ultimate kick was a printout for time. The printer is connected to the clock, and it is triggered by the navigator as the car crosses the in-marker. The clock prints out the time on a tape for comparison with the time recorded at the timing table. This is truly exotic. The owners of printouts also use them when they work on checkpoints. The printer is then triggered by a hose across the road, so that it makes an absolute record of every car that crosses the in-marker.

The move to a computer may seem terribly expensive to most beginning rallyists. The cost of a computer is a reasonable investment if you rally often for recreation and enjoy the challenge of expert competition. As we have mentioned, the computer cannot keep you on course, but it sure is a big help in solving the numerous math problems along the way. Bear in mind that the expenditure is for equipment with extremely long life: your computer will undoubtedly outlast your current and several future rally cars. In this light, and if a computer adds to your rally enjoyment, it is worth the investment. There is a healthy market in used odometers and computers too, so if your interest in rallying should fade at some date in years to come, you could recover some of your investment. We know of some rally teams who have passed their gear on to their children to use in rallying, but in any case there is seldom a total loss in the investment.

The
Time Machines

WHAT AN ENORMOUS VARIETY of clocks, watches, and timers the rally team has to choose from. Indeed, of all rally equipment, timepieces constitute the greatest array. In olden days, a team could win rallies with a wrist watch or kitchen clock, and even zero with a darkroom or kitchen timer, but those days are gone forever in championship events. The availability of stop watches, time-of-day clocks, chronographs, electric timers and clocks, digital time readouts—the lot—seems endless and it can be bewildering to the beginner. Again we urge the neophyte to use *whatever timepiece he already owns* until he learns the tricks of course-following. When he has soaked up the experiences of many rallies and tried solving their problems, then our new rallyist will know what rally class he likes to run in and what timing equipment he prefers.

You can be successful with a variety of timing devices: a pair of stop watches, one single chronograph, any combination of time-of-day and elapsed-time recorders, or the exotic electric, crystal-controlled, digital clocks. Your timing equipment will be

Heuer Auto Rally (left) and Monte Carlo (right) are excellent stop watches that can be used for rallying. Monte Carlo has the advantage of an hour counter in the center. Both clocks come with decimal as well as second markings.

a combination of personal choice for ease of use and price for ease of budget. Remember to move slowly when buying an expensive timepiece. If the choice is right, you will never need to replace it, but, if you plunge into the first watch you find, it may prove to be unhandy with your ultimate method of navigation. Perhaps an exception to this rule would be the acquisition of a decent stop watch. You can buy a good stop watch for under $25, and good used ones when you can find them are less than that. However, a really cheap stop watch (in design rather than money) with a pin-lever movement is of little value, because its accuracy is doubtful even for short periods of time. So you want a jeweled movement, and you want a watch that counts to 60 minutes. We won't quote prices on specific stop watches because the recent dollar crisis and devaluation have upset the prices (most stop watch movements are imported).

Rally supply catalogs are full of ads for watches, and a good many of them are Swiss-made. Of these, the Heuer is the most readily available over the counter and by mail order. We do not mean to imply that this one make is the ultimate in timekeeping, but we like the variety available in the Heuer line, and many watches in their catalog are well suited to rally work.

Other common makes on the rally trail are Longines, Minerva, and the Hamilton 24-hour unit which is built into a special case by the Feldmar Watch Company in Los Angeles. (Feldmar is a unique store that specializes in fancy timing equipment). The Hamilton is the classic rally clock, and it is easy to read whether in daylight or in darkness. The Hamilton movement is no longer made, but the clock is still available from Feldmar and it may also be found second hand.

The most important feature of your rally watch, other than readability, is accuracy. It must be able to hold perfect time for several hours while jouncing about in the car. It will ride in a watch clip either on the lap board or on the dash of the car, but in any case it will receive some road shock no matter how well you protect it in mounting. A good rally clock should gain or lose no more than a second in several hours.

The SOP rallyist can win with a pair of stop watches and a time-of-day device. Time of day is needed to get the proper out-times from the checkpoints, but many good wrist watches today keep accurate time and are fitted with a sweep second hand for triggering the proper out-time. Ideally the wrist watch

Master Time watch (left) has luminous dial and hands and the hack feature for time reset as well as a turning bezel. Chronograph (right) does all rally functions with a decimal and second readout, split-action second hand, and elapsed-time counter; it also gives accurate time of day on a 12-hour scale.

used for time of day will have a hack feature, which means it can be set to the second by pulling out the stem. Except when time of day is needed for restarts, the SOP team will navigate from speed change to speed change, or from leg to leg, on the stop watches. As mentioned, the stop watch should count up to 60 minutes, and if anything over a few bucks is involved get a stop watch that reads in decimal minutes as well as in seconds. You'd also like it to have a time-out device, which is an extra button on the crown that allows you to stop the watch and restart it without zeroing the time.

One good example of this keen-type stop watch for SOP rallying is the Heuer decimal timer, which is a round pocket-size watch that reads in decimal minutes and fifths of a second. It reads up to 60 minutes and has an hour recorder. The long hand reads seconds and hundredths of a minute, and the short hand reads minutes. This watch can be stopped and restarted without returning to zero; it can be used to read time of day if it is started at 12 o'clock.

Going up one step in a stop watch is the model that does all the above-mentioned chores and also has a split-action second hand. The split-action convenience costs a good bit of money, but it can be a great aid in rally work. You can punch the split-action button at a speed change or as you cross an in-marker, *calmly* read the time to hundredths of a minute from one hand (the other keeps running), then punch the split button again and the two second hands go back to running together. The split-action second hand timer is extremely valuable to the checkpoint crew for use in timing the rally; if you can afford split action, get it.

Other variations on the stop watch include the well known Heuer Auto Rally and Monte Carlo. They both come on a metal plate with screws for mounting them on the dash or on the clipboard. Like other elapsed-time counters, these also can be rigged as time-of-day clocks by starting them at 12 o'clock.

These and most windup clocks must be mounted on the lap board or the dash in semipermanent fashion if they are to remain accurate. Barney Feldmar of the Feldmar Watch Company tells us that to calibrate a watch to keep *perfect* time he must know the angle at which the watch will be running. Naturally none of the manual-wind watches are self illuminating either, and they should be mounted so that for night rallying they can be easily seen in the light from the interior navigation lamps.

The stop-watch can be used with a slide rule, and a stop watch can easily be used for leg-by-leg navigation, but when you move to a cumulative calculator or into computer rallying you will need a time-of-day watch to match your computed numbers. Heuer and other makers provide a good master time watch. In fact the Heuer is called Master Time; it is an eight-day precision clock with a sweep second hand. Heuer markets the Master Time and Monte Carlo in a package mounted on a single backing plate. The Hamilton 24-hour clock is a favorite with many for both master time and navigation. Any good watch that is easy to read and has a sweep second hand will do nicely for time of day and full navigation, but keep the stop watch handy for other problems.

The rally team which is navigating by time of day can do the whole job on one timepiece if desired, and keep the stop watch handy for off-course excursions, add-times, etc. A chronograph will provide time of day in minutes and hundredths, as well as a counting register and a sweep second hand—often with a split action—all in one device. We have used a Heuer pocket chronograph with a Curta calculator for years. The chronograph has a split-action sweep second hand, and it records elapsed time on a 30-minute counting register. It provides time of day for out-times, split action for in-times, and the sweep hand for add-times, off-course recovery and Curta navigation. And the whole bit is on one clock face. The watch was expensive when we bought it in 1964, but it is still going strong, perfectly reliable. It costs a bundle to have the chronograph serviced and it can't be done in the average jewelry store, but it's worth it. The chronograph will provide all the times needed for navigation, and the 60-second counting register can be hacked to a true time signal.

We have shown a few of the watches most commonly seen on rallies, and if it looks like a Heuer advertisement, it may be because Heuer's watches are designed for rallying. Heuer has a healthy interest in rallying, world-wide, and they have a keen catalog with 40 pages of watches for one to dream through.

No matter how fine a timepiece you use, it must be set

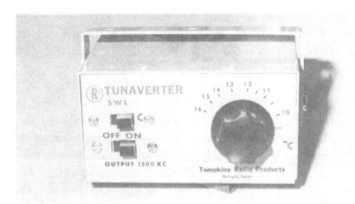

Converter to bring in time stations on your car radio is a handy gadget to install under the dashboard. Tunaverter shown here picks up both WWV and CHU.

accurately and synchronized with the rallymaster's—official—timepiece. The time source in all North American rallying today is a time signal from radio station WWV or CHU. These are no ordinary radio stations. WWV is operated by the National Bureau of Standards from Fort Collins, Colorado. CHU is operated by Canada's Dominion Observatory in Ottawa. One or the other time signal is available wherever you are on short wave radio. WWV broadcasts on frequencies of 2.5, 5, 10, 15, 20, and 25 mHz; CHU is at 3.330, 7.335, and 14.670 mHz. On most reasonably priced short wave radio receivers, WWV is marked right on the dial, so you don't need engineering training to find the right station.

Every rally we know of sets master time by these radio signals, and the novice rallyist soon becomes accustomed to the constant beep-beep signal of WWV at the registration desk, at the checkpoints, and at the rest stop. On major rallies each checkpoint crew will have a radio to insure that the clocks used are kept right on the money. WWV broadcasts a voice announcement of Grenwich Mean Time on top of every minute and transmits second pulses interspersed with announcements for the other 59 seconds. CHU broadcasts in a similar fashion with voice announcements each minute alternately in English and French. Either station is an absolute time reference, and allows the rallyist to hack his watch exactly.

Battery-powered portable radios are a common means of receiving the time signals, but we are especially fond of a little device we got from Competition Limited in Michigan. Called the Tunaverter, it is a solid-state short wave converter that allows the reception of WWV and CHU time signals through your AM car radio. The Tunaverter uses a nine-volt battery, or it can be adapted to run on car current. It is compact, merely 4 x 3 x 2.5 inches, and it will fit snugly under the dash of the smallest car. To hook it up you merely connect the supplied cable to the antenna jack of your car radio, and a multi-position switch brings in WWV and CHU through the car radio speaker. Personally, we like this method of receiving WWV much better than a portable radio. First of all, it doesn't require a search through the back seat debris to find the radio midway in the rally, and, even more important, it does not get left at home.

A rally computer usually displays elapsed time and time of day on digital readouts on the console. A clock is seldom used except for backup. Electric counters, such as the Stevens units, can be rigged so that the console display reads the time elapsed (computed time) as well as miles for the distance covered. Computer consoles are generally designed to display time; the mile counters are extras. A common setup for the nav rallyist using a Curta would be a pair of electric timers (Stevens' are solid state, oscillator-controlled, digital readouts) and a pair of electric mile counters. The team can then navigate from leg to

Crystal-controlled digital clock is the newest bit of rally gadgetry, and the coming thing for accuracy. Rallecomp's Rodon clock displays either minutes and seconds or hundredths of a minute, and it can hold a reading. Deluxe model displays both *seconds and hundredths.*

Complete Rallecomp lineup of equipment includes the Rodon clock and the set of three counters (left), the base computer with a readout for the driver (center), and the odometer corrector with an up-down counter (right) plus a WWV portable receiver.

leg (or speed-change to speed-change) or total time and mileage. Time on a computer console is often recorded on an electric time-of-day clock, digital readout also. The major advantage to a digital clock is that it is much easier to read to the hundredth of a minute than is a sweeping second hand. The round-faced clock always makes it difficult to read the minute when the second hand is in the 57 to 59 areas, but a digital clock can be copied at a glance.

An elaboration of the digital clock is the digital sports chronometer that works off the internal car power, and is quite plainly a large display digital electric clock. This is a fairly new gadget, for the rallyist who has everything else. We are familiar with just one model right now, the Rodon. The Rodon is a crystal-controlled clock with integrated circuits. It gives time of day in minutes and seconds or minutes and hundredths, and the display is large enough and lighted well enough to be read easily, day or night. the numbers are a good inch high and the readout is filtered for low glare in either red or green display. It is a simple matter to hack this clock in time of day, and its accuracy on the long haul is remarkable. The readout has a hold feature, which means you can hold at the in-marker, read the clock and record the time of day; punch it again and the readout catches up to the true time of day. The Rodon sells for about $140; it makes clock watching easy and almost foolproof.

Many of the hand-held digital electronic clocks and timers on the market read in hours, minutes, and seconds. We think these devices could function in rallying. However, we have had no experience with them, so we wonder. They may be too big and heavy for dashboard mounting, and we've read that their batteries are only good for about four hours of continuous use—not too keen for an all-day rally. As a rule the hand-held electric digital clocks and timers seem to be designed for use as stop watches primarily and would be difficult to make work as time-of-day clocks. Two clocks we have seen zero every time they are punched, and that could be a disaster on a rally. And these timers seem quite expensive (listing at close to $200), so we think right now that the rallyist would get better service for the price from an old-fashioned wind-up chronograph. However, that's probably going to change. Crystal clocks *are* the new generation of accurate timepieces. Watchmakers say that in 10 years anyone who needs really accurate time will be using the crystal electric system. We expect the second generation of these devices to be less costly as well.

You see that there is no end to the variety of clocks and timers you might find useful in rally navigation. Eventually you will discover just the right combination of dials and readouts that fits your nav system perfectly. Just get as much experimenting done as possible before buying any of the clocks that run into real money. It would be really neat if you could rally with an expert or two before you make the final choice. You may find that digital clocks are just what makes the game easier, or you may prefer to work with a round dial. Do make every effort to use them all on the road before you squeeze the budget to buy your rally clock.

Zeron 440 computer has good-sized readouts for every function. Digital clock (left) is certainly easy to read.

MERCEDES BENT

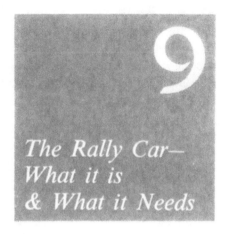

The Rally Car—
What it is
& What it Needs

THE RALLY CAR is the third most important part of the rally effort, and the team that gets serious about the sport must give some thought to the type of car for the competition. Also, there are a few inexpensive gadgets that are a tremendous aid to the rallyist and legal in any class he might decide to run. As mentioned earlier, the vehicle can be anything that holds two or more people and rolls on four wheels, so long as it is street legal. Some of the most successful rally teams compete in the most mundane type of transportation, but rallying is a sport and certain types of cars adapt more easily to the rigors of rallying than others.

We have personal preferences in cars, as do most people, and our favorites are compact-sized and nimble on the road. The full-blown land yacht from Detroit can be rallied with no problems though. A few years back one California team did the entire National Championship series in a Chevy Sport Van. This budget-strapped team drove all over the country to rally, and saved money by camping out in the rally car instead of staying in motels. You can see that any vehicle can cope with the TSD rally, but as you get deeper into the sport, you may want to change to an automobile that is more pleasant to drive on winding back roads than the full-size sedan. In this era of two or more car families, one car is often an import or Detroit compact, and the rally team will probably end up using that vehicle.

We think the ideal rally car should have several features, box stock, that the driver will need on the road. Good seats come first to mind. You want fast acceleration values, good brakes, a high degree of reliability, and above-average forward and side visibility, but a comfortable cockpit and front seats is most important. Any car that has reclining seat backs on front buckets gets really high points as a rally tool. The rallyists spend a good deal of time in those front seats, and the average bench-style seat can become pure torture after the first few hours on a rally. The reclining device is good for comfort for the team, and also good for extra space needed for the Texas-sized body. Anything like a seat recliner that aids comfort in the car will lessen the fatigue factor. The uncomfortable or tired team is far more prone to make mistakes than the less annoyed competition in a more comfortable conveyance. We place seating comfort as the first priority in choosing a rally car.

The next item we look for is a reliable configuration and something that is mass-produced. Really exotic cars are great fun to drive, but cranky electrics or mysterious engine problems are a real pain in the middle of a rally. We recall one time standing in the aftermath of a rain squall in the wilds of west Texas, trying to find a Lotus Elan's distributor cap so we could dry it off. The distributor cap was somewhere down under the Weber carbs and attendant hardware, and every hundredth of a minute we spent by the side of the road looking for it was one penalty point. We took a healthy maximum penalty on that leg. It was just swell to have such a fine car, but we would have quickly sacrificed the keen but complicated sports car for a more reliable, well proven, and easy-to-service drive train. And we always like a rally car to have a full distribution network in the United States. You never know where the rally scene will take you, and it is nice to know that if you have car trouble

98

there is a sales and service dealer for your breed of machine *somewhere* in the countryside. Maybe you only need a speedo cable, but you *need* it.

After comfort and reliability, then we consider the performance of a rally car. A good rally team can compensate for a small-engined stone of a car, but with the wide variety of cars available today on the U.S. market, you may as well have decent performance. You don't need a drag strip screamer for acceleration values, but what you do need is an engine/gearbox combo (and it doesn't matter whether the gearbox is manual or automatic) that will allow you to gain time on the road or entering a checkpoint. An off-course excursion on the route can put you down a minute or so on that leg, and if you recover the course quickly, you still have a chance for a zero. The rally car should be strong enough, and handle well enough, so that on a route calling for, say, a 45 mph *average* the driver can run fast without undue strain or danger. Some small-engined cars take a good bit of time to build top speed, and many of them just won't hold 65 mph uphill. A nicely strong engine is excellent in some checkpoint situations also. Suppose you are on a sign hunt, slowing from the quoted average to peer at signs, and find you are half a minute down. You round a corner and see a checkpoint—with a zippy engine you can boot the car, and gain a good bit of the time back before you cross the in-marker. The healthy small-block V-8s of the early 1970s are ideal for solving this problem.

Good brakes go without saying in any car the thinking driver might buy, but some models have exceptional braking, and it doesn't seem to relate to price or brand all that much. The car should have the best brakes available for its type to handle all the normal, on-road rally situations. For example: "Was that the sign?" "Dunno—I was calculating." A screech of brakes, a quick reverse to verify the sign, and you are back on the route. (You will look in the mirrors, won't you?) You might like to have a quick slow-down in front of a checkpoint also, because some teams run a bit early, up to one quarter of minute, and then slow violently when the in-marker is spotted before proceeding sedately into the control without snagging a penalty for creeping. SCCA National Rallies usually require a brake stop test, from a slow speed with hands off the wheel, as part of their technical inspection, and the official may tell you to have the brakes adjusted before you start the event.

Last, but certainly no less important, you must be able to see out of the rally car. Route instructions are clued by landmarks and signs, and most general instructions call out any sign or landmark visible while approaching or passing it as eligible for use. Extreme wrap-around windshields often have a good bit of distortion, especially at the corners. This makes a hard-to-see sign—especially at night or in the rain—even more difficult to catch, and that is one type of problem you don't need to carry in the rally car. Good side window visibility is important too, as you will discover. Some highly styled sportsters are nearly impossible to see out of from the side.

Beyond these general points, the rally car should be selected for personal reasons: how it fits into the budget, its work-a-day value to the family, and just plain whimsy. Make it a car that you really like, whether for its looks, or because it is your favorite brand, or whatever the reason. We stress personal preference because you are more apt to take extra care in appearance and mechanical maintenance on a car you really like rather than basic transportation. We have rallied in a wide variety of cars—in everything from trucks to Minis—and found good and bad points in them all. Although the price is outrageous, we love the Porsche 911 we are currently rallying. We find that its handling, general performance, and super comfort are ideal for our schedule, which includes everything from local TSD events to the SCCA and FIA pro rallies that use both unpaved and paved roads, high-speed tests on closed roads, as well as pure navigation problems.

We have been observing the types and brands of cars at rallies for some years, and, although they change a bit from year to year, they do fall into three groups of car styles. We see sports cars (GT), Detroit pony cars, and small sedans. The most common car is any type of Datsun: hordes of 240Zs and 510/610 sedans are in evidence everywhere. The Z's popularity in all segments of motoring is a miracle of the 1970s, and the Z-car rally teams just love those cars. The Datsun sedans proliferated in rallying primarily because Nissan USA has for several years offered prize money to private owners who run Datsuns in SCCA rallys. The Datsun award program is explained

more thoroughly in Chapter 12, where the various championships are described. In the west the Ford Capri is quite popular,
as is the Ford Pinto and the Chevrolet Vega. Beyond that, the
choice of sedans spreads evenly to Toyota, Volkswagen, Saab,
Mazda, Opel, Subaru, and so forth, depending on the section of
the country in which the rally is held. The buy-American group
heavily favors the pony cars; Mustang and Camaro lead that
pack by a healthy margin, and properly optioned they make
good rally machines. Many Mustang drivers went Ford a few
years back when Dearborn had a rather extensive rally support
program (since gone the way of most competition support from
Detroit). The sporty Fiats and Alfas have a big following. Many
traditionalists stick with British Leyland. And there are always a
few Opel GTs and Corvettes on a big rally.

The Santa Monica Sports Car Club offers some statistics on
the brands and colors of the 90 cars that showed up for their
First Friday Niter rally in April of 1973:

By Brand:

Ford	19	Fiat	5
Mustang	9	MG	5
Pinto	6	GT	2
Maverick	2	Roadster	2
Falcon	1	1100	1
Cortina	1	Porsche	5
Datsun	13	American Motors	3
240Z	6	Mazda	3
510	4	Triumph	3
610	1	Oldsmobile	2
Pickup	1	Toyota	2
Roadster	1	Austin Healey	1
Volkswagen	11	Alfa Romeo	1
Chevrolet	10	BMW 2002 Tii	1
Vega	3	Citroen	1
Camaro	2	Dodge van	1
Corvette	2	Mercedes Benz 280SL	1
Chevy II	1	Mercury	1
Impala	1	Plymouth	1
Chevelle	1	Pontiac	1

By Color:

Blue	17	Silver	4
Red	13	Gold	4
Green	12	Brown	3
White	11	Grey	2
Orange	9	Bronze	2
Yellow	6	Beige	2
Black	5		

The Santa Monica club concludes that the average First-Friday-Niter rallyist drives a blue Mustang, but you can see that there *is no* average rally car. It is true, however, that enthusiast-type cars do dominate in rally circles; we think it is because the folks who like a nifty car also like to do something with the car, so they go rallying.

Whatever the car choice is, eventually the owner will have to buy some rally tires. Many sporty cars now come with steel-belted radials, but in any case such a tire is a requirement once the team gets serious about measuring mileage. Steel-belted radial tires do not expand or change diameter with speed, friction, and heat; they do not, therefore, affect the accuracy of the speedometer. Most expert rallyists are fanatic about these tires. Michelin (the pioneer manufacturer of radials) is the most favored brand; it is a rare TSD championship event that finds the winning car wearing anything but Michelin steel belts. Today many other brands of steel-belted radial tires also have an extremely low expansion factor, but the Michelin has the mystique. At any rate, this type of tire is needed to maintain a constant odometer correction factor throughout the rally. On major events the odometer check leg will have a tire warm-up run, to get the tires heated to normal road temperature before the measured mileage check begins. The general instructions will usually say something like this: "The course was measured with a 1971 Datsun equipped with an electro-mechanical odometer driving from the left front wheel. The tires were 165 x 13 Michelin ZX, inflated to 26 psi cold. The weather was dry and clear with temperatures ranging from 70 to 90 degrees F." It seems terribly technical, but the expert rallyist will then know a ball park measurement ratio for his equipment against the rallymaster's mile.

The reasoning behind the need for non-expandable tires is simply the need to run the odometer check, figure the odometer correction factor, and calculate the entire rally on that one factor. A conventional cross-ply tire expands and contracts with changes in temperature (changes in pavement surface will change the heat in the tire). The resulting change in rolling radius would produce a wide variation in odo readings, too much to be accurate while measuring to the hundredth of a mile. However, the type of tires on the car need not concern the novice until he learns how to stay on course. Only then should he go into his wallet for non-expanding tires, auxiliary odometers, and whatever equipment he desires.

There is a lot of rally equipment available, although it may seem unavailable to the beginner shopping in the local speed store. Watches and calculating devices are covered elsewhere, but some goodies are useful almost from the start no matter what rally or what class you may choose for the competition.

Because a high percentage of beginner rallies are run on Friday night, the team soon learns that it takes one of the navigator's hands to hold the flashlight while he marks off the instructions with the other hand, and he still needs a free hand to turn pages, rifle back through the GIs, and so forth. The extra interior light, a reading lamp if you will, is the first thing we would recommend for a rally equipment purchase, and you can buy or build in almost any price range. Some firms, like Lucas, make a goose neck, 12 volt light that can be fastened to either the car or the clipboard. Discount houses carry lamps that plug into the cigarette lighter, but watch out for those: the bulbs don't last very long—only about two hours on the average. Budget watchers should check mail order catalogs like J.C. Whitney to find inexpensive map lights (under five bucks). Ours from the Whitney catalog is built on a swivel mount and it plugs into the car's 12-volt electrical system. It mounts anywhere there is space, and we found the very same light on the Capri decor package. Some rallyists prefer a light aircraft cockpit light, and we agree that it is nice to use, with both a red and white filter, but these lights are relatively expensive unless you live near an aircraft wrecking yard, or have a good surplus store in the area. Some sports cars, especially the British-built ones, come with a map reading light, which is handy for the novice

Aircraft cockpit light (top center) makes a superb navigation light for the rally car. Comes with both white and red lenses. The compass is a big help on any rally, but necessary in the midwest.

team. We have rallied with everything from 45-dollar Grimes lights to truck clearance lights tacked on the window center post, and the red lenses really ease the bounce and windshield reflection that can bother the driver and impede the search for signs in the night. The vast majority of rally teams rig their own interior lights to suit their needs and the interior design of the car. All you need is something the navigator can read by that doesn't bother the driver. Any white lamp can turn red by spray-painting the bulb or fitting a red lens over the tip. The newcomer can get all sorts of ideas just by checking out other cars on a night rally.

We think, and many experts agree, the next purchase for the team should be a lap board. Most of these clip or lap boards are homemade from a piece of wood. Some rally teams mount the odometers, the watches, and so forth on the clip board, but it makes a very heavy item in the navigator's lap. Plus the dangling wires for the odo connections might cause unnecessary strain on the cables. We like to put odos and clocks on the dash and illuminate them with a soft rosy light. The clip board we use holds the calculator, the route and general instructions, the log, and the scratch paper. No matter what you do for a lap board, a good tip is to keep it lightweight. Even more important is to back the board, whatever it is made from, with foam rubber to

A reader board is a must for any serious rally team. These SOP experts are checking off completed instructions as they wait for an out-time on the next section.

keep the board from sliding around in your lap. If the lap board starts to slide during a hard turn on the road, the whole section of calculations can be lost, and the spongy backing on the board will keep it well stuck to the navigator's legs. For design ideas, check again on the rally cars in your area. You probably will never see two boards exactly alike, but you can sift the design theories around and come up with something that works for your team.

A reader board, sometimes called a reader box, will become a must as the rally work gets serious. Route instructions are generally provided in standard letter size sheets, and flipping pages has caused more than one error on a rally. A reader board is quite simply a pair of rollers, usually with a light behind the center. The rally instructions are taped together, end to end, and then taped on the ends to the rollers. As you go down the route, you can read the instructions in one continuous roll by turning the roller knobs. This device is another one that is often manufactured at home, but it is available from Stevens Engineering in California and doubtless from other rally sales outlets around the country. Mounting a reader box on the center dash allows both driver and navigator to check the route instructions without the need for conversation, which might disturb the delicate calculations going on in the right seat. We

HOW TO MAKE A READER-BOARD

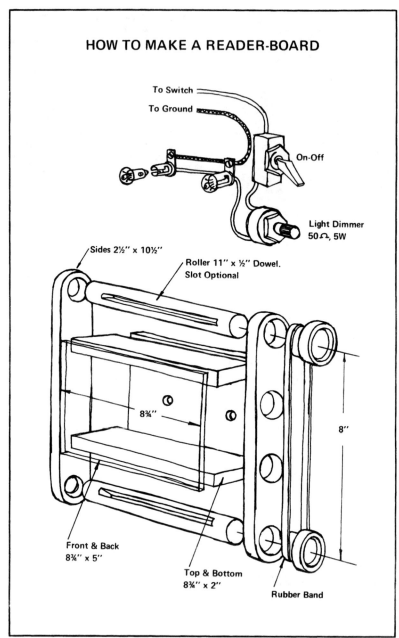

To Switch

To Ground

On-Off

Light Dimmer
50 Ω, 5W

Sides 2½" x 10½"

Roller 11" x ½" Dowel.
Slot Optional

8¾"

8"

Front & Back
8¾" x 5"

Top & Bottom
8¾" x 2"

Rubber Band

Light box is made of plywood, ¼-inch for the back and ½-inch for everything else. The front window is ¼-inch translucent plastic, clear or red.

To use reader-board, tape route instructions together end-to-end. Insert the ends in top and bottom roller slots (fold the corners). Or just tape the ends to the rollers. Roll the instructions down onto the bottom roller to start. Put rubber band over knobs to keep tension on rollers. Roll instructions toward top as needed.

Equipment for Class A need not be elaborate. This Capri has a home-built reader board, the Halda Twinmaster, one stop watch and one master time clock. Factor cards are under navigator's left hand, and she is correcting average speeds on the route instructions. Driver is re-reading the generals before the start.

Yu-u-ck! What a mess. The equipment is actually better than it looks—a computer, pair of counters, front-wheel odo, all the good stuff—but the wiring job!

Here you see the full deck, the works, and a trim installation it is. See all the nice black boxes, so clean, crisp, and efficient. How can you go wrong? You'd be amazed.

consider it a must for any team after the first few rallies, and well worth the investment: very little when home built, or about 24 bucks from Stevens.

Other convenience items depend a lot on the interior design of your car. In olden days, cars had right hand door pockets, usable glove boxes, and similar spots to put things in. Depend on losing the use of the dash-style glove box if you go into odometers and the mechanical class of rallying, because that is the place to put that equipment on most cars. The center console box is very handy for stowing spare pencils, maps, and so forth, but a map pocket by the navigator's right foot is keen for the route card and maps as well, and can be easily fabricated. A tight fitting sunvisor on the right side is good for holding the generals and the route card also. We like the sunvisor better than any door pouch because things can drop out of the door pouch when the door opens. If it's your route card that drops out of the door pocket and you don't realize it, you will be in trouble for a score at the next checkpoint.

A styrofoam cold drink cup makes a fine pencil and clip

holder, and it can be glued, taped, or stuck in the proper place. The same type of cup can also be tacked under the dash to hold a flashlight. Each rally team develops gadgets for its own needs, and creative engineering will blossom after each event when you wonder why you didn't have this or that on board, located differently. Anything you feel might have ruined your zero on a leg will get redesigned.

In many areas of the country rallymasters will use the points of the compass for instructions..."Turn north after Stop." If this is a local practice, an effective compass should be an early addition to the rally gear. As with all rally equipment, the beginner should observe what others are using before rushing out to buy the first thing on the list. Quite often it is more fun, and far more convenient to make your own bits and pieces to fit your car.

Checkpoints

THE MOMENT OF TRUTH in any rally comes as the car and team approach a timing control, or "checkpoint." There are numerous varieties of checkpoints, but the vast majority of timing controls are called "open controls." The location of an open control is unknown to all but the workers.

The open control is used on every type of rally described in this book as well as on many events that we have ignored. On an auto rally, an open control or checkpoint is the basis of the competition and scoring. Cars are timed from control to control, or leg by leg, and each leg is a mini rally of its own, in that time lost on the leg is lost forever when you enter the checkpoint. You will receive a score on that leg, and be given a new time of day to use for zero time on the next leg. Most general instructions will state that time lost on one leg cannot be gained in another. The reasoning behind this theory is obvious. It just wouldn't do to have a stream of rally cars bombing along public roads on a Sunday afternoon trying to make up time that was lost through some mistake. The urge to regain a chunk of lost time on a leg is further discouraged by use of a maximum late penalty at each checkpoint. The maximum is usually two to five minutes (200 to 500 points). If the instructions say that "max" is five minutes and you're 10 minutes behind, don't sweat it—and don't race—the maximum penalty (5 minutes) is all you can lose. The rallyist's jargon is "We took a max." If you're more than fifteen minutes late (or early) there will be a "missed checkpoint" penalty, but that is usually only about 100 points more than a "max."

The location of an open control is not given in the route instructions. Your first knowledge of the location is visual, and by then you are committed to entering the timing zone at the quoted average speed. The control will be on the right-hand side of the road, and it should be in an area where there is ample room for several rally cars to pull completely off the road and park. Physically the checkpoint consists of three or more stations of workers. The first station is located by the in-sign; it is manned by someone with a signaling device. A paint spot on the pavement or some landmark dictates the precise spot for timing, premeasured along with the entire rally route. The car is timed when the front wheels pass that spot, generally referred to as the in-marker. When the front wheels pass the in-marker you will hear a voice yell "Mark!" or a whistle will blow and perhaps a flag will drop. These and sundry other methods are used to denote to the timers the exact moment for timing the car.

The second station is the timing table. Depending on the average speed at that point in the rally, the timing table will be far enough from the in-marker to allow an easy stop for the rally car. At the timing table the in-time is recorded on a master log sheet; here the rally team must stop, but usually remain in the car. A checkpoint worker will provide you with the time, either by marking it on your route card or by handing you a timing slip. No matter what the method, there will be two new times written down for you to digest. One will be the time of day when you crossed the in-marker; the other will be your departure time from that checkpoint. Allowances for dead time (the time spent between the in-marker and the out-marker) vary from two to several minutes. Three minutes is about average, but if the cars stack up the last car will have five to ten minutes

Checkpoint location must allow room for the checkpoint crew and room for a string of rally cars to pull off the road. (See top photo.) The location shown at bottom is lovely but poor as a checkpoint.

to wait. Each car is assigned out on its own minute, just like the start, so if five cars all arrive in the same minute at a checkpoint, the workers will separate their out-times by a full minute each, giving the first car a three-minute dead time and the last in the group a seven-minute dead time.

The out-marker is the third station on an open control. It is generally unmanned, and it will be 50 yards or more down-course from the timing table. At the out-marker everyone starts fresh, with a new time and mileage for the coming leg. The out-marker, like the in-marker and other signs throughout the rally, will be identified by the club initials or a rally symbol. The out-marker may also contain such important information as the word "OUT," the average speed for the start of the leg, and the instruction number. If this information is not given on the out-marker itself, it will be given in the slip handed out at the timing table. The rallyists may also be given the total mileage to this point (as a handy reference to the navigator), and may be told to skip a number of instructions. The instructions skipped may have been eliminated due to some late-occurring route problem, or, more likely, they may apply only to those who missed the checkpoint and need to get back on course after a trap. Each rally team times itself out from the out-marker. It is not wise to cheat and leave early, for there may be another control just around the corner.

Of course there are a number of variations on the open style of control, but they all contain the three essential functions of an in-marker, a timing table, and an out-marker. It is common to see both time and mileage discounted from rally calculations for the area between the in-marker and the out-marker, but either time or mileage, or both, may be listed as official in the general instructions. The time, of course, is set by the timing table, and would add to your time for the next leg; the mileage could be cumulative for the whole rally.

Some clubs will allow a longer period of time for the cars entering and leaving an open control, and they will perform the additional function of scoring the cars or passing out true times to that point so the team can instantly see its score on the preceding leg. A common method of keeping score is on a control card carried in the car. It is the competitors' job to keep track of the card in the car and keep it handy for presentation at the checkpoint. Actual scoring methods are covered elsewhere.

Because the Sunday rally will have eight to a dozen legs, it takes a good-sized work force to man all the checkpoints. Rallymasters in small clubs have devised another way of building-in a time check for additional legs, particularly useful after a trap. This is the Do-It-Yourself checkpoint. The DYS checkpoint will be called out in the route instructions, usually on a numbered instruction. It might read like this: "Execute a DYS at 'SANTA ANA 14'." That means you must time yourself into and out of a leg, and the point of action is a "SANTA ANA 14" sign. (You know it is a sign because it is in quotes.) The location will contain enough off-highway space for a number of cars, and the GIs will have told you to add a minute, or whatever amount of time, to your true time at a DYS. This time allowance gives you a chance to stop, calculate your true time to that point or just read it from your watch, and then continue on the route without too much panic. At the DYS you must write in your arrival time in the first available "in" spot on your route card. Then you add the stipulated time to that number, and write in your out-time on the next leg "out" slot. This is one of many instances where you should have an accurate time-of-day watch, since these times are recorded in time of day. When you reach the next manned checkpoint, a worker will seal your time notations by use of clear tape or a wax pencil so that later you cannot alter your time for that checkpoint.

The passage control is also a handy type of route check for the understaffed rally committee. It can be manned by just two persons—one in a real pinch—because it is not a time control. The workers record car numbers only. Like any checkpoint it will be in an area where it is safe for several cars to stop off the highway. The rally cars stop and have their passage recorded on the route card or on a log, usually on both. The time used in a passage control is compensated for by add-time. The add-time may be given in a handout, or the out-marker may refer to a numbered instruction which calls for a two-minute add-time at each passage control. Rallymasters use passage controls for many reasons; the main reason is that they make possible additional checkpoints without the need for timing equipment.

Sometimes the passage control is a secret or hidden control, where the workers spot and record the numbers of the cars that pass, and there is no need for the rally team to stop. This type of checkpoint relies heavily on the workers' ability to spot the car numbers, and they are not favored for championship events. Monte Carlo-style rallies, in Mexico particularly, use secret controls for timing, but this style is a no-no in the rest of North America. There are several points against them. The first is that no serious rally team will stand for a timing control where it is not possible to check the time recorded on the car's passage. The champion rallyist has a number of clocks, and he knows to the hundredth of a minute what his time was when he passed the in-marker. He insists on being able to check the timing at the timing table. It can happen that the checkpoint has a clock error, and more than one rally leg has been saved by the timing equipment in the first car. If the rallyist is an expert, and he feels the time call was wrong, he will point out the need for a radio time check on the clock in use, and at that point the workers will adjust their clock to National Bureau of Standards time, broadcast on radio station WWV. Another reason for not using secret timing controls is that they require that the car numbers be large enough for the control worker to read them from afar, which means they are also large enough to attract attention from the local constabulary, and the thinking rally-master tries to avoid that.

A passage control can also be used as an off-course control, one which is designed to turn lost rally cars around and get them back on course. Without some sort of device to collect them, wayward rally teams might go many miles off course before their mistake became evident, if ever it became evident. Club rallies may cover this problem by posting a sign that may say "Club X NO" or "GOOF" to tell the teams they are off-course. But a high-caliber rally will use the off-course control instead, providing there are enough workers to go around. When you enter an off-course control, your route card will be marked, and the checkpoint log will mark your passage for penalty points to be added to your score. Next you generally get a handout that calls for a U-turn and gives you an instruction number to pick up the course from after your goof.

The open timing control is predominant in all time-speed-distance rallies. Most common on the in-marker is a flagman or somebody yelling "Mark!" At that sound the navigator should note his time. The leg time is recorded at the timing table on the in-marker man's signal. (The novice will check his watch to see that it is accurate with the time he gets from the worker, and the expert will check for the opposite reason.) The total leg time will be recorded in time of day, which is the only method of timing the rallyist should be concerned with in modern times. Time of day is an absolute with time signals coming from the National Bureau of Standards radio station WWV. It is handy to have a watch reading elapsed time for the leg timing, add-times, and so forth, but time of day is the first order of priority on rally timing.

The checkpoint should be in position, ready to work, as much as half an hour before the first car is due. At least 15 minutes before the first car is due, the checkpoint team will begin recording every minute that passes on the log. The timer will be ready when the first car appears, and at that time he need only to read the fractions of a minute on the watch. One worker records time, another spots the car number to be assigned that time, and a third acts as runner at the timing table. It seems like too much help, but each person can be extremely busy if several cars appear in the same minute. Procedure varies, but usually the runner goes to the stopped rally car, picks up the route card, and returns to the timing table where in-time is marked on the card. An out-time is assigned, marked on the card, and recorded in the log. The double recording of in and out times allows the rallymaster to score from the logs as well as from the route cards, and it can also be handy for checking a route card that may look to be altered. Few people will attempt to re-make their time on their route card, but in the rush of the rally the card can get dirty from being dropped in the mud, having coffee spilled on it—any number of similar disasters that make the times illegible. Carrying the card in the car is favored by most clubs, because the rally is then self-scoring, and trophies can be awarded quickly at the finish rather than after a long wait for the checkpoint crews to arrive. The control log is used only for judging protests.

The open control may also have an automatic in-marker, something developed to the best of our knowledge by Southern

California rallyists. It's really very simple: a sort of hose is stretched across the road, just like the bell-ringer at a gas station. When the front wheels of the rally car run over the hose, the car is timed. In simple systems, a bell or buzzer sounds and the timing table records the car's in-time. In more sophisticated systems, an electric clock prints the time on a tape—in hundredths of a minute. Neat. All the timing table worker has to do for a log is write the car number on the print-out. The standard log and watch is kept around for backup in case of a battery failure or some other technological crisis.

The checkpoint crew and location do not happen haphazardly. The organization of the checkpoints is critical to the success of a rally. An otherwise perfect leg may have to be discarded from scoring if the checkpoint is in the wrong place, missing altogether, or just plain inefficient. One slip of a time call on one car, and the whole control will be eliminated if that rally team catches the mistake. The checkpoint crew will consist of a leader, called captain, and a few workers, of which at least one timekeeper should be fully experienced. The runners can be the novice workers who learn the operation of the control in easy stages. The whole crew arrives at the point of action either by pre-arranged instructions from the rallymaster, a marked map, or by following the course-opening car along the route. Most common way of finding the control is by means of written instructions from the rallymaster. On all day rallies one crew normally works at least two control points, possibly more, depending on the geography. The smooth functioning crew will be set up with all workers on station when the course-opening car comes through, at least 15 minutes before the first car is due. Ideally each checkpoint has a WWV receiver to keep the watches right on, but if not the course car will check clocks before proceeding down course. On major rallies the sweep car will close the checkpoint and pick up the log from the crew. On club events the crew may close down about half an hour after the last car was due, or when all entries have passed, then head for lunch and another location or head for the finish.

Equipment needed for working a checkpoint includes suitable clothing for any type of weather from excessive sun to pouring rain. Light clothing with rain gear and a warm jacket stowed in the car is the general mode of dress, and comfortable shoes are a must. Sunburn lotion and insect repellent are handy in the summer, and snow boots and really warm clothes are needed in the winter. An ice chest or a thermos of your favorite non-alcoholic beverage is good to have, and it usually saves everybody time if you pack your own lunch along.

The actual checkpoint devices are the responsibility of the captain, who will bring the signs, the timing units, flags, hose, card table, radio, logs, paper, and pencils. If poor weather is expected, the checkpoint vehicle can serve as the timing table to protect the workers and the clocks and paper. Vans with side-opening doors are really neat for working checkpoints. Any car can be used for the timing table on a night rally where interior lighting is a big help, but the more spacious van is really ideal.

Any description of checkpoints should include the Monte Carlo or stage-type rally timing controls. On a stage rally the competitors can arrive early but are penalized for arriving late, and there is seldom any dead time or mileage in the control. Cars may pass the control and park, and the navigator takes his route book, control card, or whatever it is to the control table. He waits out the time to the proper moment, and then presents his time card for the stamp and the time write-in by the official. The stage rally runs on a time schedule and all times are pre-assigned, so that lost time in a leg must be regained to avoid further penalty. The challenge comes in making the times over difficult roads, arriving in enough time for the navigator to jump out of the car and present the route card on time. Instead of the official stamp, some rallies use a time clock at the control; this is common in International Championship events abroad.

Club-style Monte Carlo rallies combine the pre-assigned time schedule with a little TSD work. The rally car can run early until it reaches a "stand-off" point, a mile or so from the control. (The exact location of the control is unknown.) The trick here is to leave the stand-off point with enough time to arrive on-time at the control, which is known to be in the next mile or so, but one must navigate on TSD to zero the leg. Once they report to the time control, the rallyists then move up the road to the out-marker. A rally worker at the out-marker ensures that the cars do not leave early, but that they do leave on or after their preassigned out-time.

So there are many styles of rallies, but the checkpoints remain pretty much the same. The checkpoint is always on the right-hand side of the road so that it's easy to get in and out of. It will be around a curve so that the competitors can't see it until their car is into the timing zone. Once the rally car is in sight of a checkpoint, creeping (well below average speed) is frowned on, and an outright stop will bring a heavy penalty. The TSD rally car is supposed to be on time all the time and thus ready for a checkpoint whenever it occurs. A good control requires more than a wide spot on the road. A control might be located near the site of a difficult instruction in order to catch the teams before they can correct a time error. A control location might be chosen for ease of access by the workers, or perhaps for its parking area. The number of cars that might arrive at one time has to be anticipated in order to be sure there is room for them all without causing any traffic hazard. A turnout on a mountain road is ideal. Where it is is what all the contestants would like to know or be able to guess. The challenge of meeting all these requirements and hiding the location goes to the rallymaster.

Rallies differ from racing in the methods of timing, in that the shortest time is not necessarily—seldom, in fact—the winner. The winner is the team whose elapsed time on each leg is closest to the perfect/ideal/true time established by the average speed. A rally may have a restart in the middle of the day, where time and mileage are zeroed and one starts anew. This does not happen in racing. Inasmuch as checkpoints are responsible for timing the individual legs of a rally, the timing and even scoring chores are spread through a host of people working in different locations. It is a complex organization on a major rally, and it is a credit to the sport that few problems arise from checkpoint mistakes. The people, like most rally people, are dedicated and willing workers, and they have little to gain from the experience besides the satisfaction of doing a job and contributing to the success of the event. The unwritten rule of rallying is to always be pleasant to the checkpoint crews. They seldom know the route and can't help you with your problems, but they are working hard. Keep your anger inside the car, and smile!

Becoming a Rallymaster

AS THE NOVICE BECOMES PROFICIENT in rallying, he will get involved in putting on his own events. The job is far more complex than it appears on the surface.

The proper organization of a rally requires competent help at all levels. The first-time rallymaster would do well to work as co-chairman on a club or beginner event a few times before plunging into the solo organization of a rally. Rallymastering is a learning-by-doing process, and the duties are much more easily handled by the man or woman who has helped out on several events before tackling a complete rally on his own.

When you are ready to plunge into a rally organizer's chores, begin with a short event such as a Sunday run or a Friday night rally—one with a running time of four hours or less. There are certain problems to face that are constant on any rally, but logistics is far more simple on the shorter rallies and fewer workers are required. The first thing to do is to choose the starting area, the finishing area, and the general direction of the route. Pick a starting area that has easy access for the teams you hope to attract. It should be a spot convenient in travel time and large enough to accommodate the cars expected without interfering with normal business. Shopping center parking lots offer large areas that are relatively vacant on weekends. They are in favor as starting points because full facilities, such as a gas station and a restaurant, are usually close by. Areas behind banks and other non-weekend establishments are good too. Always have a gasoline station nearby, because most contestants will want to start with a full tank, and it is nice to have restrooms close to the start as well.

After locating a starting point, the next step is to find the finish. Then sit down with detailed road maps of the area and chose your direction of travel. Aim for a rest stop or a lunch stop midway on time in the rally, and find the route back to the finish area from there. Check approximate mileage on the map, and start considering the average speeds anticipated. Be sure you are not making the route too long in either miles or time or both. Do all this before you leave the kitchen table and the maps. We hope you have been rallying for a year or two in the vicinity, and if so you should have a good idea of the available roads and how they connect to one another. You will have had first-hand experience on what makes a good starting location, rest or lunch stop, and finish facilities, and you should have several possibilities in mind. Trace your general route on the map and get it fairly well down on paper before setting out on a survey trip. Our local expert rallymasters choose the locations of the start, lunch, and the finish before they go anywhere.

Now the rallymaster and his navigator take to the road with the maps and notebook. They will motor through the countryside picking out the course and noting all usable signs. At this time the rallymaster should have determined how difficult the rally will be with respect to course-following and math problems, and therefore spot the loops that could work into a good trap. Don't try to make the traps too complicated. Novice rallymasters often try to throw everything they know into the first event, making the rally too long, too fast, and too difficult to follow. Any one of those factors can ruin a good event; in combination they can set rallying back for some time in the area. At any rate, the first on-course run should set the actual course and determine the odo check leg, the roads that will be used, and whether the rest stop area is OK. The rallymaster should always check with the manager of the coffee shop and the gas station at the rest stop area selected to be sure they will be open on rally day. Most restaurants appreciate knowing the time of day they can expect an unusual influx of business, and many will put on extra help to handle the rally trade. Also on the first run through the rally route, keep the eyes peeled for good checkpoint locations, and note these on the log. Drive through the course at comfortable speeds, but just find the course on the first round.

Don't try to modify the general instructions to suit the existing roads (that's another common mistake of the novice rallymaster). It's too easy to overlook something that may cause a whole leg to be thrown out from the rally. It is best to start your first event using existing general instructions. In other words, write the rally to conform to GIs that are in common use by a local club or council. This practice can avoid a number of real problems that could ruin your first rally. By all means select or write the general instructions before doing the route. Revising the generals to suit a particular route instruction often leads to a real goof on another leg of the rally. Doing the generals first is a good rule, and almost a necessity on a championship event.

Once the route is more or less set in your mind, make another run through the course picking out the signs and landmarks to use for speed changes and course-following, and check again for control locations. Now is the time to pick out your goof loops; try to place them close enough to a control to make them valid—close enough, for instance, that it would be impossible to regain the lost time or lose the early time before the checkpoint. Beware of using temporary signs, such as billboards or signs pointing to housing developments. Temporary signs can exist for years, and then vanish the day before the rally. The same warning applies to home-built signs: local folk have a way of tearing down your signs or, maybe worse, altering them in fiendish ways. So stick with bona-fide, permanent-style signs, like street names, highway numbers, and historical landmarks. There are plenty of these anywhere, and you will then eliminate the need to post a bunch of emergency signs. Every run through the course should be recorded on paper—or use a tape recorder if you run it alone. Remember to stay realistic on average speeds. As the rallymaster becomes more familar with the route, he begins to think the speeds he originally picked out are too slow. They usually are not, and it is only the prior knowledge of where the signs occur that makes the rally seem too easy. Raising the average speeds after the rally is set is another common mistake, to be avoided by any rallymaster, whether it is his first or fiftieth event.

You will probably make as many as three trips just setting the course. Then you will make a trip to actually write the rally route instructions, and this will take a bit of time. Go slow and get it right; check spelling, check that sign locations are according to the generals, and so forth. Now you are ready to measure the mileages and confirm the speed changes. You should measure the miles with non-expanding tires and a hundredths-counting odometer. If your car is not so equipped, borrow one that is to avoid errors in measurement. On each trip, and this one too, pay special attention to your checkpoint locations. Be sure there is room off the road for the cars to stop, and make every effort to keep all controls away from congested areas.

Back home, type the route instructions, and do proofread them carefully. Use an adding machine, calculator or similar device to figure the true times from your mileages and average speeds, and have someone else double-check everything. At this point in development your rally is ready for a checkout. Remember, when you type the route instructions, make a few carbon copies and use the copies for the check run. An SCCA championship rally makes a checkout mandatory, and it is a fine idea for any event large or small. Cajole a friend or some of your control workers to do the checkout on your rally. It is important to do the check ride on the same day of the week and at the same time of day as the rally schedule. This factor will provide a simulation of traffic conditions prevailing on rally day; you may need to lower the average speeds or insert an add-time in congested sections.

There are sundry methods of running a checkout, but two cars can handle it easily. The rallymaster and his navigator can either follow the checking car, or run ahead of it and set up the control locations. The route checkers invariably uncover a few

126

errors in the instructions, or, if not errors, vague areas that could conflict with the general instructions. Discuss these problems sensibly with your checkers, and don't be afraid to clarify an instruction that you thought was perfectly adequate. Do your rewriting on the spot so that the signs in question are in view at the time. Contestants will still score penalties on that leg, so go ahead and write in a redundant instruction, because you do want to keep the rally on course, or at least on an off-course loop. If there are a number of changes or clarifications, get another checkout before rally day. If there are no changes, your master copy of the route has been proofread under rally conditions and you can be sure it is accurate. Don't retype it. It is very important to use the same bit of typing for the route instructions on rally day as those that were used for the checkout ride. Gremlins can creep into a retype job; beware of that.

With the route done, you may think that the rallymaster's chores are over, but that is not so. Actually there is other work that should be going on while you are setting the route. If your first event is a club rally you can call on the club members for checkpoints and other work areas. You need to select a checkpoint chairman or captain and he makes an excellent choice for your first checkout crew; he may spot a possible problem in a control location that didn't occur to you. Don't be afraid to delegate *authority* to your workers; you can't do it all yourself and retain your sanity. Do keep in touch with all your committee heads, and be sure you have enough competent people and equipment to handle the controls. Each control needs watches, signs, a radio, logs, and so forth. Check the chapter on checkpoints for the entire operation of that part of a rally.

You will need to have all the logistics taken care of long before rally day. The trophies and the dash plaques, or jacket patches, or whatever memento goes to the entries, have to be ordered well in advance. Previous club events will give you a ballpark figure for the quantity of plaques and trophies to order. Some club rallies provide only the mementos at the rally; the trophies are presented at the next meeting. This practice avoids the ordering of too many or too few trophies.

Make the entry form simple while providing all the needed   127 information: names, addresses, type of car, class, and so forth. Be sure and get at least one mailing address from a team no matter how small the rally. It is nice to mail out complete results a few days after the event, and near impossible to provide them for all on rally day.

Most SCCA rallies require some additional paper work to conform to national SCCA rules, and a championship rally requires a good deal of paper work between the rallymaster, his local region, and the SCCA headquarters in Denver, Colorado. For this reason most SCCA national championship events will have two honchos: a Rally Chairman and a Course Marshall. The Course Marshall is actually the rallymaster—the man who lays out the course and does all the instructions. The Rally Chairman takes care of all the paper work, the sanction requests, the ordering of trophies, the selection of a rally headquarters, and the details of meeting all the rules and requirements of a championship event. A big rally requires some advertising, flyers—and detail work beyond belief. There is so much detail work on an SCCA Championship event that sharing the work makes a lot of sense. We took on the job of Rally Chairman on an SCCA national a couple of years back and spent so much time on the logistics of the rally that to this day we have never seen the actual course or know any more about it than the general direction. But the SCCA championship rally is no place for the novice rallymaster. By the time you are ready for a big event, you should have plenty of grass roots experience.

On your first rally you will need a registrar at the start and two folks are better than one. Don't tie yourself down with that job. You will need a master time clock and a WWV radio receiver at the start too, and it is handy to have one worker taking the entry fees and assigning starting numbers and another passing out instructions. Be sure you have everything loaded in your car before you leave for the starting point. You will need a folding table and chairs, and possibly a light for your registration desk, boxes for the dash plaques or whatever, the route instructions and the general instructions, car numbers and so forth. Have plenty of route instructions, all stapled in sets, and extra copies of the general instructions. A beginner rally generally provides both sets of instructions at the start; a

128

championship event will have the generals mailed to all pre-entries. Make plenty of copies of both sets of instructions. You never know how many cars your rally will draw. We have entered more than one Sunday rally where the club had to turn away entries because they ran out of instructions by car No. 100.

You will need a team to work as starters: one man to send the cars on their way at the proper out-time and another to round up the stragglers in the parking lot and get them lined up in numerical order. If you have a big entry, it is a good idea to have a sweep car (the team can easily be the same as your starting team) to follow the last car around the route, close the checkpoints, and pick up the logs. The rallymaster usually opens the course for the simple reason that he knows it better than any of his workers. Besides it gets him away from all the contestants' questions at the start. He should start out a good half hour before the first car is due to leave and check the course carefully for any sign changes. He should be prepared to post emergency signs, and have enough people and equipment in tow, either in his car or following, to man a checkpoint if the workers have not arrived by the time the course opening car goes through.

When the rallymaster arrives at the finish, normally located in or near a restaurant parking lot, he then makes sure the room he arranged to house his awards presentation is ready for occupancy. Many pizza parlors and bowling alleys have meeting rooms or banquet areas that work well for this purpose. It keeps the rally teams out of the main stream of the restaurant business, and the contestants still get to eat pizza, drink beer, and chatter about rallying while they tote up their scores.

The scoring team aids the rallymaster in checking all the route cards at the finish; the efficient team will start scoring as soon as the first route card is turned in. If this habit is followed, it requires only a shuffle of the route cards to find the winners when the last car to finish has turned in his card. If there is a question or a protest, the sweep car should be in with the checkpoint logs by that time, and a check through the logs will generally take care of any timing protest. Route protests are something else, and they may be resolved with an instant decision by the rally committee. Or it might take a physical 129 check on the area in question. Some championship rally results are held up for weeks while a court of appeals considers the protested leg. This sort of thing holds up the trophy awards, at least in class if not the entire rally, so the thinking rallymaster tries to avoid the complicated route instructions that might be subject to differences in interpetation.

Eventually the trophies are all awarded to the winners (and it

is a nice touch to give a small trophy for Dead Last). Your first rally is over, and a few things went wrong. As you gain experience in the rallymaster chores, things will still go wrong, but it won't bother you as much. With experience you know how to handle any problem. So if you have to throw out a couple of legs on your first rally, do it gracefully, and remember how it happened so you can avoid it on your next event.

Writing a good TSD rally will get easier each time you do it. Remember to keep the route short, keep the speeds low enough to allow for sign reading, and keep the course-finding problems within reason. Our local experts have the rallymaster business down to a fine science, and people all over the country have the same resident experts. In southern California, a rallymaster will spend about four days on the road to write a Sunday championship rally. Two trips will set the course and write the route instructions; one trip will set the mileages and nail down the average speeds. The fourth trip is a personal checkout before the club checkout, and it's always done after the route instructions are typed. The experts advise the beginning rallymaster to go over the course several times before writing the instructions, but warn against becoming so familar with the route that signs and landmarks not mentioned in the instructions become relatively invisible.

Rallying is fun for the participant, and writing a rally from scratch is even more fun. It does take a good bit of time, but, like any other achievement, it is rewarding to be at the finish of your own event and listen to the teams praise a certain section or, even better, compliment you on a good rally. With any luck your entry fees will have covered your out-of-pocket expenses on trophies, gasoline, and so forth. You should keep competing as well as writing rallies to keep current with the state of the art. After you chair a few club events, you might want to tackle a championship rally. Be sure you have plenty of trusted workers for a biggie, and you will enjoy writing the championship as much as a Friday night run.

Classes & the Championship Rallies

12

AS THE SERIOUS TSD RALLYIST becomes more proficient at the game, and his home begins to fill up with trophies, he begins to look for new worlds to conquer. How about a championship title at the end of the season? It is a rare city that doesn't have a rally club or sports car club council running some type of championship series of events. If there is no such thing in your neighborhood, find the closest SCCA region: they undoubtedly run a rally series. Also, many states have a state title at the end of the year. Anybody who has a championship at the end of the year runs events all during the year. Guaranteed.

The rally series most available to the average rallyist is the city or county championship. We have found some differences in the rally codes issued around the country, but they all have the same purpose. That purpose is to organize a series of rallies in one geographical area with classes to suit and separate the majority of local contestants. Most common is a three-class system for the year-end points winners, and these three classes

133

may go by such names as Expert, Navigational, and non-Navigational, or Senior Nav, Junior Nav, and Seat of the Pants, or quite simply A, B, and C. In Class A/Expert, there are no restrictions on navigational aids: you can use any kind or number of gadgets you want. This is the class for teams using computers and those teams using Curta calculators and similar cumulative counting devices. The middle ground, Class B, varies most widely in rules around the country. In general, B or navigational entries are allowed to use auxiliary odometers, slide rules, rally tables, and so forth, but are specifically barred from using any cumulative calculators. In some parts of the U.S., Class B cars may carry the same fancy equipment as the A cars, but the team rather than the equipment is classified. In other words, one win in the middle class will put that team into the A or expert division, regardless of how much or how little equipment they have. In this case, the purpose of the B class is to give beginning nav rallyists a place to compete without fighting the experts.

Class C/SOP is the largest class as a rule, and it is the spot for the budget-minded competitor as well as the beginner. SOP rallying is something a good many teams develop into a fine art, working only with a pair of stop watches and pencil and paper. In most rally series, the SOP car is allowed to run the odometer leg, but at the end of the check, the odometer section of the speedo is taped over by an official. The SOP team may calculate their speedo error on the odo leg, but from that point forward the whole rally is run on dead reckoning for time, speed, and distance, with only watches and paper and pencil for aids. Some clubs allow the use of factor tables in Class C, but most do not; normally any such aid will move the entry up one class. Rallies where a high percentage of the entry is expected to be in the SOP class are often written without the timed or mileage turns favored by the experts. In some areas, a different set of instructions is given to the Class C cars. In these rallies, every effort is made to separate the SOP cars at the start from the nav cars, because it helps the continuing effort to keep the clever SOP runners from bird-dogging or taking a mark from a computer-equipped car.

Often a local championship event will include a fourth class for beginners. The entry form will state that you must really be a beginner with no winning scores in your background. The beginners category is designed to get more teams into championship rallies. On the west coast SOP is a very popular and highly competitive class and a rank beginner would not have a chance. So the beginner class provides an introduction to championship events, with the same route instructions, full freedom of equipment, and trophies to be won.

State championship rallies are generally run on the rules of the strongest regional council of clubs. In some places the SCCA rally regions are strong, and the state title series will use SCCA club and divisional events as well as non-affiliated local rallies for the points-counting competition. Other regions, such as New England, may combine several states into an area championship, and still others, such as California, may not have a state title series at all. California has both a Southern California and a Northern California Council of Sports Car Clubs; both have a championship series. The same is true of the Central California Rally Council and Associated Rallies (also in Southern California); they both have a title series each year. The size of the state (both area and population) and the interest in rallying produces the great number of rally titles which the local competitor can garner.

Normally the championship rallies are purely amateur events: the winners receive only trophies. Of course, enterprising rallymasters sometimes are able to acquire sponsorship, often by promoting the rally in conjunction with a local festival. Some rallies offer cash or merchandise awards, and in some areas the sponsor provides free gasoline on the route. But the task of acquiring financial help for a time-speed-distance rally is a tough one, for there are no spectators and few performance factors visible to entice a prospective sponsor.

The Sports Car Club of America, through its more than 100 regions, is by far the largest single factor in the sport of rallying. SCCA runs a full program of club level, divisional, and national rallies, and in 1973 introduced the pro rally series. Each SCCA region is a club on its own, involved in the full spectrum of sports car activity: racing, rallying, slaloms, time trials, and even concours and car shows. The larger regions in the heavy population centers tend to concentrate on amateur and professional road racing, leaving the rally business to a hard core of 135 rally enthusiasts within the club. Some unabashed racing regions farm out their rally organizing to area clubs not affiliated with the SCCA. However, the average region runs club level rallies for members and guests, and these may be TSD, gimmick, Monte Carlo, or just a gaggle to a picnic. Unlike racing, rallying seldom has an SCCA regional championship; the regional rallies are generally part of an area or council championship series.

The SCCA divisional rally is the first step towards a national championship effort by a rally team. The SCCA is divided into seven geographical divisions for administrative work and for amateur racing. The divisional rally program is an offshoot of a similar racing format. It came into being a few years back to encourage more SCCA rallying and to develop more national championship-caliber rallyists in all corners of the country. Divisional rallies are covered in SCCA's booklet, *Rally Regulations,* and even more detail is available in the club's giant-size *Rules for Organizers.* The divisional rally is fairly open for local custom with the exceptions of classes, sanction permits, and general rules of the road. To qualify as a divisional, usually a one day rally, the event must cover a road course of not less than 150 miles and enforce the SCCA safety rules on the cars. The rules are simple and make good sense. Each car must have working headlights, parking lights, stop lights, turn indicators, horn, windshield wipers, and brakes. The tires must show decent tread; there must be a rear view mirror. Each car must carry a tow rope, first aid kit, road flares, fire extinguisher, and have seat belts. The vehicle may be anything that is street-legal in the state of registry. Entrants need not be members of SCCA, but if they do not belong to some region of the club, they are not eligible to earn championship points. They do qualify for trophies and any other rally awards.

The divisional rally is good training for the national rallies, both for the competitors and for the organizers. The rally may reflect a number of local customs, but they must be cleared by the checkout crew and the SCCA Divisional Rally Steward. Other than some modifications of the general instructions to comply with the SCCA national regs, a divisional rally differs very little from the average council event. The rallies generally run on Sunday, they last six or seven hours with a gas stop and a lunch break, and trophies are awarded. Some divisions crown class champions at the end of the year. For rallyists who are interested in the national championship, the divisional affords an opportunity to pick up some extra points.

The SCCA provides two divisional and national championship classes, labeled simply A (equipped) and B (non-equipped). Class A cars have no limit on the navigational equipment allowed and correspond to the Expert cars listed above. SCCA Class B cars are allowed the use of rally tables, slide rules, and watches, and they may also use one resettable, but noncompensating, odometer that counts up to tenths of a mile. Specifically barred in Class B are compensating odometers (adjustable for error) and cumulative calculators, but the one legal odo may be added or relocated for the navigator's use. All *computing* devices from the Halda Speed Pilot on up are illegal in Class B.

For the 1973 season, the SCCA Rally Board adopted a non-mandatory, non-championship Class C or SOP, but noted that it was an addition to be used at the organizers' discretion and to be scored for championship points within Class B. Entrants in Class C are allowed to use the stock vehicle odometer in the stock location, paper and pencil for calculations, and conventional timekeeping equipment. Specifically barred in the new class are tables, slide rules, or similar calculating devices.

The SCCA also provides for two categories of rallies. Divisional and national rallies may have either an open sanction or a club sanction. The difference between club sanction and open sanction is in the amateur status of the rally and has no effect on the championship points earned. With a club sanction, entrants may compete only for trophies and points; the rally may not award participants cash or items of intrinsic value on the basis of their finishing positions. If the rally is in the open category, there is no restriction on the value of prizes or cash awards. Competitors in an open rally must apply to SCCA for a competitors license, for which there is a nominal fee.

An open sanction costs the organizing region more because SCCA's fee is higher. The higher organizer's fee for an open event compensates SCCA for a sponsor's promotional use of the event, but the fees are low enough to encourage rallymasters to find sponsors for the big rallies. Because the entrant is running for cash or merchandise, the SCCA feels he should pay a fee.   137

Any advertising on a rally car must be approved by SCCA. The permit costs about $25 a year. But sponsored cars are a small segment of the SCCA rally scene; most rallies are run in the club category—no money, no sponsorship.

The National Rally Series is the big league of TSD rallying, and the Sports Car Club of America is the only group with a truly national series. Classes and general rules are the same as the divisional events, except the route must cover at least 400 miles and take two days to do it. There are rules providing for suitable rest stops, and for an eight-hour break in each twenty-four hour period. Route instructions and general guidelines for national rallies are well defined in the *Rules for Organizers,* and there is a great amount of detail on what is and isn't allowed on a national. The strict control of the rally rules at this level is an effort to ensure that the serious points hunter might go anywhere in the United States and find a national rally that runs to the same set of rules they use at home. The use of route-following conventions is spelled out in the SCCA rally regs, and local "cute traps" are frowned upon.

Championship points are awarded equally to Class A and Class B, driver and navigator, on national and divisional rallies. There are no bonus points for an overall win. A national rally awards 10 points each to the class winners, 8 for second in class, and so on with a diminishing scale that ends with 0.2 points for 25th in class. Divisional rallies give exactly half the points of a national for the same finishing positions, and the points go only to paid-up members of the SCCA.

If a rallyist gets serious about going for the national title, he needs to prepare a budget for the year and pick his events carefully. Generally council and state championship rallies are one-day runs; they seldom call for a long-distance drive or overnight accommodations. However, the SCCA title-seeker must run at least five nationals, of which no more than two will be reasonably local. The budget must cover at least 2½ days food, lodging, and gasoline for each national, plus the time off from work needed to make a Friday night registration hundreds of miles from home base. Our five national rallies, to take an example, could include two in the Los Angeles area, one in San Diego (130 miles away) and two in Arizona (about 500 miles away), but we should run a couple more for insurance. The western divisionals can run into a lot of travel also. Distances between rallies within a division are not as great in the eastern part of the country, but the travel time is about the same and lodging often costs more.

The rewards from SCCA rallying are modest: a big trophy for the top points people and a rookie-of-the-year award for highest points by a first-year SCCA member. So fun is really the only reason to do it. However, some manufacturers of cars offer cash rewards to those people who rally in their brand of vehicle. The manufacturers' interest was awakened about 10 years ago when SCCA began to offer a large trophy every year to the manufacturer of the automobile that gained the most points in national rallies. Chrysler was the first American factory to enter a team of cars in national rallies. They started with a full team of Chrysler 300s and ended their participation with a single Barracuda, but they were rewarded with the manufacturer's title every year from 1963 through 1966. Chevrolet won it in 1967, aided by folks rallying everything from Corvettes to vans. Volvo took the honors in 1968 by sponsoring just one car. At this point of development, several manufacturers jumped into the game with money—contingency cash which they paid to rallyists who owned and drove their brand of automobile. Ford, Saab, Volvo, Porsche, Renault, and Datsun come to mind as companies who paid cash awards in national rallies. Ford used to split up a ten-grand pot each year among owner-drivers of Fords on the basis of the total number of championship points they accrued during the year. Ford also fielded a team of three Mustangs with hired drivers, and naturally took the individual and manufacturers titles in 1969 and 1970.

Datsun won all the marbles in 1971 and 1972, and the national and divisional rallies are filled with Datsun cars today. The reason is simple: they pay money. Datsun has a very comprehensive system of cash awards which they pay to rallyists who are driving their cars, whether old or new. They firmly avoid paying so much as a penny for sponsorship of any driver in particular. However, many Datsun dealers sponsor rally cars, and the dealers claim a direct sales result from it and from the parent company's rally program. Datsun's money is paid right after the event, upon presentation of the official results to   139 their Competition Director in Los Angeles. Here's what they paid in 1973:

	national/divisional
1st Datsun to finish	$100/60
2nd Datsun to finish	75/40
3rd Datsun to finish	50/25

These awards are given in both classes, A and B. Datsun also gives bonus awards in national rallies:

1st overall in a Datsun	$200
2nd overall in a Datsun	125
3rd overall in a Datsun	75

There are also year-end prizes for the top point-getters in Datsun cars, and there's an award to the Datsun rallyist of the year. That's nice, but it's the rally-by-rally cash that really comes in handy, because it enables a winning crew to run more events out of their home area. The money won on the last rally goes a long way toward paying for the next one. Other manufacturers have awards programs from year to year, but none is so deeply involved in the SCCA national rally championships as Datsun.

The year 1973 may go down as a landmark in U.S. rally circles because the SCCA established the Pro Rally Series. These are high performance events, along the lines of the European national rallies that produce drivers for international championships all over the world. The emphasis is on car preparation and driver ability. Before 1973, the Mony Series of off-pavement winter rallies in Michigan, Ohio, and New York was the only such series of rallies in the country. With prodding from such pockets of enthusiasm around the country, the SCCA Rally Board took the step toward another national championship. The Rally Board says that the purpose of the Pro Rally Series is "to encourage participation in and the support of, on a national basis, rallies offering a driving challenge." However, safety and state regulations are held to be of key importance in staging these events. The SCCA Rally Board (headed by Wayne Zitkus) purposely kept the pro rules fairly loose to allow for local conditions and make use of whatever back roads are available for off-pavement stages or speed tests. Devotees of high speed rallying are few, located mainly in the northern climes, and SCCA wanted to produce a series that would interest performance rallyists in all areas. They also wanted a series that would draw sponsors and provide the scene for budding international rally drivers to learn their profession. Rally cars racing on special stages against the clock could very well appeal to a host of performance-oriented drivers for whom the restrictions and expense of amateur racing are just too much.

The Pro Series was no sooner announced than both Datsun and Saab posted contingency awards for the series. Datsun's dough comes after each rally, as in the nationals, but goes only to first through third overall (these are one-class events). They pay $400, $300, and $200 for 1-2-3. They also pay year-end bonuses to their top point people. Saab's support program includes $200, $100, and $50 for 1-2-3 in a Saab, plus year-end money for first through third in pro rally points, provided 75 percent of the pro rallies were done in a Saab. We expect other companies will join in the contingency business, and we look for the manufacturers of parts such as spark plugs, brakes, and so forth to join the pro rally series also.

The competitive pro rally car can also be driven to work. Any car that is street legal is eligible to run—and that includes four-wheel-drive vehicles. Roll bars are required on a number of the events, and will doubtless become mandatory as the series grows. Any number of driving lights are allowed on the special stages, and car modifications, such as skid pans, are encouraged. Engine mods are not mentioned in the rules, which really means the cars must be streetable but not necessarily street *legal* today. In other words, the safety inspectors will be looking for things like roll bars and fire extinguishers, not air pumps and catalysts. All cars must carry a current street registration.

The SCCA Rally Board defines a pro rally as one that follows a stage rally format, meaning that it will consist of short, high-speed, driver-test sections connected by a series of low-speed transit runs. Cars start the driver-test sections at least one minute apart. Low time there will be very important in determining the overall winner. The transit runs are to be free of traps, since they serve mainly to link the special stages together and allow for food and gas stops. Course-following is made as easy as possible: mileages are given on every instruction, there are course arrows, and there are confirming instructions at all action points. The rally is for the driver; he will display his (her too) performance on the special stages. The road is closed to normal traffic for the occasion. Both driver and co-driver are required to wear safety helmets, and any intersecting roads are blocked to local traffic for the time of the rally's passage. The architects of the pro series recommend that cash awards replace trophies on these rallies, and they advise using a seeded starting order based on the team's previous performance in this type of rally. A championship award has been established for both driver and co-driver; the winner is determined by a points system based on the total number of cars starting in each event.

While the SCCA recommends the stage format for the pro series, it does leave the door open for rallies without special stages, and for rallies with other types of tests. Some of the 1973 events will include stages, map work, and some TSD running. Unlike the pure TSD rally, the high-performance rally (which of course will have some TSD and navigation work in it) can be conducted on an old airport or some other easily controlled road, and the real performance involves holding a 45 mph average while running a slalom course past time controls on the corners. Some rally organizers have gotten permission to use private roads on private property, thus ensuring the absence of any traffic other than the rally cars. The opportunities are endless for speed tests or stages that are safe (relatively), legal, and demanding.

Naturally the pro rally driver has a heavy investment in his car. He needs only a set of counters and a calculating device for navigation, but he does need driving and fog lights, skid pans, and some tuning and tinkering on the drive train, plus a roll bar if he plans to do the whole circuit. However, there is money to be won from the organizers as well as the contingency money, and if your fun comes from driving hard on back roads, usually in poor weather, the pro rally series is your game. We do think that it is the one type of rally that will eventually attract some major sponsorship for the sport in the USA, and we look forward to the day when we can send an American crew to Europe to compete with the best drivers and cars in the big time, big buck, international rallies.

Professional Rallying & the International Set

BIG LEAGUE RALLYING means the international championship series—which is as big in rallying as the worldwide Formula-1 series is in road racing. While it is seldom of interest to U.S. sports writers, international rallying has a tremendous following in Europe. The news media there are heavily involved in rally coverage, and auto manufacturers spend more money and time on their professional rally teams than they do in racing. There are more than a dozen events on the world championship schedule, and two dozen firms directly, *heavily*, involved in the sport. Ford of England, for instance, will spend more than half of their competition budget on rallying in 1973. They estimate that the value they get for their money is about 50 percent development of their production cars and 50 percent image building for the marque. Performance rallying is a popular sales promotion device; the car companies believe that it proves the durability and performance of their street machines far better than racing does.

The glamour events on the circuit are the Monte Carlo Rally

and the East African Safari. The Monte draws a huge entry every year, more than 300 in some years, and it is famed for having starting points all over Europe. Cars from 10 cities in Europe—Reims, Oslo, Marrakech, Athens—converge on a common route to the Riviera; the top 60 or so are then selected for the mountain speed tests where the winners are established. Generally, only the factory teams will survive the snow-packed roads in the mountains. The speed tests are really races. They are run like hillclimbs and time trials, where each car starts on its own minute and races against the road and the clock rather than wheel-to-wheel with other entries.

The East African Safari is a rough desert course, fanning out in all directions from Nairobi. The rally teams struggle through rough roads, desert sand and dust; many of them succumb to the mechanical problems peculiar to the desert. They also face the hazard of colliding with the colorful—and bulky—wild animals that roam freely around the rally roads.

The top glamour events on the international calendar have been the truly long-distance events. First was the London-to-Sydney Marathon, run late in 1968. It started in London, wound through Europe and the Near East to India, then by boat to Australia and around that country before the finish at Sydney. The Marathon took a month and covered more than 10,000 miles. It was won by a Hillman Avenger from the English factory. Two years later the World Cup Rally was run, sponsored (like the London-to-Sydney) by a British newspaper. This one started in Wembley, near London, and finished at the World Cup football games in Mexico City. The route went from England through Europe and back to Lisbon; by boat to Rio de Janeiro; south, and then west, and finally north through South America; across the Panama canal and on to Mexico City in just 40 days. Ford of England won with a team of very special Escorts.

We have seen how the sport of rallying came to life in this country after World War II, and we know that the speed test and its attendant hazards quickly faded from popularity as the highways and byways became crowded with traffic. However, several tiny corners of enthusiasm for the high-speed rally managed to keep active. U.S. enthusiasts practiced the art of performance rallying in Canada, where the Shell 4000 and the

Canadian Winter Rally became top attractions. It is no accident that many performance-minded U.S. rally people (and clubs) live in the states bordering Canada. The Canadian rallies are run on unmade roads in the rain, snow, and mud of late fall, winter, and early spring.

The Canadian Winter Rally, organized by the British Empire Motor Club is a three-day bash through the deep snow, ice, and sub-zero cold in February. The rally starts and finishes in Toronto (there's an overnight stop in Ottawa) and it runs all over the bleak and frozen back roads of northern Ontario and Quebec. Only the hale and hearty should attempt this. It is FIA-sanctioned, and runs FIA Groups 1, 2, 3 and 4 as a rule. Canadian, American, and overseas manufacturers have entered teams of factory-backed cars in this grueling run; the Canadian Winter Rally has long been a prestige event for rally nuts. The average speeds called for are impossible for the road conditions, and the route is well marked by the burning red flares of competitors digging out of the snowbanks.

The Shell 4000 Car Rally was a 4000-mile run sponsored by Shell Oil of Canada (at a cost rumored to be around $250,000 per year). The Shell usually started from Vancouver and wound its way across Canada for six or seven days toward Montreal, the finish. The overnight stops were brief, and the rally team

averaged up to 18 hours a day on the road. The Shell carried international championship status for a few years, and did attract the stars and cars from Europe. The British came in force: BMC, Rootes, Triumph, and Ford of England shipped cars and drivers to the new world. From North America came Chrysler, Ford, American Motors, and even Chevrolet with teams of special cars and hired drivers. Detroit's participation was "secret" (except for that of Ford, who were open about it) but made evident by the tramp-tramp-tramp of engineers on the rally trail across Canada. The format of the Shell Rally varied greatly from that of the European rallies. The Shell included plenty of average-speed sections and tricky course-following just like a TSD rally. But there were at least half a dozen special stages (speed tests on closed roads or race courses), and some really brisk running was needed to cover the 4000 miles.

The last of the classic Shell 4000 Car Rallies was held in the spring of 1968; it went from Vancouver to Halifax. The winners (both from Michigan) were driver Scott Harvey, a Chrysler engineer, and navigator Ralph Beckman, a math student. They won in a Plymouth Barracuda, making it an all-American win. Shell of Canada retired from sponsorship of the event, supposedly because of poor press and advertising results. A trans-Canada rally was organized a few years later, but all efforts to bring back the glamour (and sponsorship) of the old Shell 4000 have met with little success.

For 1974, the Ontario-based Rally of the Rideau Lakes has been granted full international championship status by FIA. The Rideau Lakes Rally will bring a world title event to Canada for the first time in several years. Plans are afoot to move 1974's rally from May to October, preceding the November running of the Press-On-Regardless Rally in Michigan. This will allow the European teams to make one trip across the Atlantic and compete in two championship events in two weeks.

South of the border, rallying is a different game again, but there are active rally clubs all over Mexico. Two FIA-sanctioned rallies draw U.S. entrants, mostly from the southwest and Texas. The International 24-Hour Rally produced by the French Club of Mexico is the prestige run. It is a three-day rally starting on the Friday night, usually in July during the rainy season. The format includes high-speed transit zones, a couple

148

of short special stages, and many short—timed to the second—
TSD sections. The rally runs mostly on pavement; only about
30 percent is on dirt roads. The interesting part of this rally lies
not in the special stages, but rather in keeping tight to the
average speeds on hazardous mountain roads in the outback
that are usually wet. On the TSD sections all controls are secret,
something most U.S. and Canadian rallies do not permit, but
the timing is usually accurate. The Mexican 24-Hour Rally is a
tough one for Americans to win, since the customs are different
and there is some language barrier on the road for most, even
though the instructions are printed in English. SCCA champions
Roger and Kathy Bohl in a team Ford Mustang won the rally
outright in 1970. They won about $2500. It was their first year
on the event, and the only U.S. win in 16 years of the rally.

In September, the RAC Club in Mexico runs a similar event,
called the RAC Mil, which is also FIA-sanctioned. This rally
offers similar prizes, plus free hotel accommodations to all
non-Mexicans in the entry. The RAC Mil winner is decided by
the TSD sections, although the rally does have a special stage
run on the grand prix race track on the outskirts of Mexico
City. If the organizers were to change their format a bit to
match the Press-On-Regardless and Rideau Lakes rallies, a
Mexican rally could easily become the third world championship
rally on this side of the Atlantic.

The big time in the United States today is the Press-On-
Regardless Rally out of Detroit. The POR, as it is known, has
been run in November for 24 years. During that time it has been
organized as a club event, an SCCA divisional, and an SCCA
national; in 1971 it became an FIA-sanctioned rally. The POR
used to be a 24-hour, straight-through run, but it recently
evolved into a few nights of rallying with rest stops during the
day. (The rough back roads carry little traffic at night, and
whatever traffic there might be is easily spotted by the
approaching headlights.) In 1972 the goal of all dedicated
performance rally types was achieved, when the POR became
the first FIA international championship rally held in the
United States. The work involved in organizing such a rally is
tremendous, even though the rally is confined to one state,
Michigan. The members of the sponsoring Detroit Region of the
SCCA and the Ralligators Club have devoted years in the per-

formance rally field to attain the skills and knowledge needed to get the job done.

The moving force behind the POR is the small, less-than-50-member, Ralligators Club. This hardy band of Detroit-based enthusiasts became a club in 1961, when members of the Volvo Owners Club in Detroit made up a team entry on the Canadian Winter Rally. They adopted a watch-toting alligator for their emblem. Teams of Ralligators have been entered in every performance-type rally in the north-central states and Canada for over a decade, and they have clung to the organization of the POR for the big U.S. event of the year. A few years ago Leonard Oil Company (later known as Total of Michigan) began to sponsor the Press-On-Regardless, donating money and free gas to the organizers and competitors. This financial help enabled the Ralligators, with the sanction of the Detroit Region of the SCCA, to produce the international championship rally—four days and nights of competition—in November of 1972. The route went through woods and over back roads from Detroit to the Canadian border. Unfortunately at season's end, it drew only one team car from Europe, the Lancia of Harry Kellstrom and John Davenport. Lancia had already cinched the 1972 world title. The Lancia led the POR for some time, as expected, but midway on the 2000-mile route it lost an argument with a Michigan birch tree. The ultimate winner of the rally was a Jeep, which was a surprise and somewhat of a shock to the devotees of pure, sporty-type, rally cars. Jeep's two-car, factory-backed team of four-wheel-drive Jeep Wagoneers came in first and third overall. Their win has occasioned a great controversy over the eligibility of four-wheel-drive vehicles on FIA rallies, and the controversy is not settled yet. The winning Jeep was driven by Gene Henderson, a Dearborn police officer who had been instrumental in founding the Ralligators club. It was his third POR win in 15 years of rally competition.

But the important news for U.S. rallyists came in 1973, when the Sports Car Club of America announced its Pro Series: a championship rally series featuring high-performance stages run on back roads and dirt roads. Like the Monte. SCCA figures that the national series is mainly a participant sport, like amateur racing, and will remain at the same level of interest in years to come. The club had been under pressure for years to back the POR and provide a series of similar rallies all over the country. Now they've done it. The idea is to school drivers for international events, and also to allow the manufacturers some reason to be interested in the performance of their cars. The Pro Series is all one class, and the format is loose enough to provide organizers some latitude in setting up the special stages and other performance tests, while allowing contestants to improve the performance of their street machines. Less than six months into the program, some of the rally organizers have already been successful in acquiring sponsors for their events, and they offer cash and prizes.

Stage rallying is becoming a national sport via the pro series. There will be regional differences, but the emphasis is on performance (of both man and machine) on the special stages—speed tests, time trials—whatever the name. As we said in Chapter 12, the stage is usually a dirt road, and one that is easily closed to traffic for the hour or so that the rally passes through. Cars are started a minute apart on the stages and timed at least to the second or more often to the hundredth of a minute; the quickest time gets the lowest score. Stages average from four to ten miles in length, and usually all cars run in the same class. For this type of competition, horsepower should be combined with agility in order to get over the rough roads or the snow, or whatever the obstacles. The stages are connected by either elapsed-time sections or straightforward TSD legs to link the stages and allow for food and fuel stops. Route instructions on all legs are clear and easy to follow, normally clued by statute mileages, and often contain extra confirming information and tulip arrows.

Tulips are the unique course arrows which originated on the Tulip Rally in Holland years back; they are in common use now. The rally car is always on the tail or ball of the arrow, and that is the point where the quoted mileage should come up. The arrow describes the intersection and points in the intended direction. Tulips are handy in any rally, but they are particularly good in the wilderness areas used for stage rallying because usable signs and landmarks seldom exist there.

A variation on the stage-type rally involves average speed sections instead of stages. It is used because some states frown

TOTAL MILEAGE	INCREMENT MILEAGE	INSTRUCTION	SIGN	TULIP
46.28	0.33	NARROW BRIDGE		
46.41	0.13	Keep Left - D.L.O.	McKINLEY REDUCE SPEED	
46.56	0.15	Right at STOP	STOP 600	
46.90	0.34	Keep Left		
47.75	0.85	Keep Right		
50.59	2.84	Straight		
51.25	0.66	Keep Left (CAUTION)		
51.30	0.05	Control 8S. Take 16 min. to reach Control 10S at 63.57 miles. Stage #4 "RUSSELL"		
51.76	0.46	Keep Right		
52.90	1.14	Control 9M "RUSSELL"		
53.26	0.36	Straight - CAUTION		
54.76	1.50	Left at T		
55.81	1.05	Right at T onto pavement	STOP	
60.99	5.18	Straight on M-65	Junction M-72 M-65	
63.40	2.41	Right	SUNNY LAKE RD.	

Example of "Tulip" Route Instructions.

152

on closing public roads for "races," and the legality of such closures is doubtful even if local officials approve. So the organizers pick out a challenging piece of road and assign an impossibly high average speed to that leg. The speed chosen will always be under the legal speed limit, but one will probably have to run faster to keep up the average. The rally road may be a muddy single-lane trail through the woods, on which the assigned average will be perhaps 45 mph. The fastest car may be only a few minutes late on the leg, and the stage winner is the team that acquires the fewest late points. You see how challenging it can be. The dirt road, the snow, and the stage type rally appeal to the driver who likes to run hard and fast on lousy surfaces.

Car preparation plays a big part in success on these rallies. Roll bar and helmets are required, as well as first aid kit, fire extinguisher, flares, etc. Exterior lighting is free of restrictions. Most cars run two spread-beam lights, two pencil beams, and two fog lights; the lights are nearly always quartz-halogen type. Many competitors favor aircraft landing lights, but use quartz-halogen headlights as well. The rooftop spotlight is not legal under FIA rules, so most teams avoid use of this device (it is usually illegal on public roads anyhow).

Scott Harvey—three-time winner of the Press-On-Regardless, winner of the Shell 4000, as well as being victorious on a number of other stage rallies—offers us some tips on car preparation for stage rallies. He runs in Michigan and Canada primarily, so his ideas are slanted toward special-stage roads that are narrow and lined with trees. Scott feels that size is important in choosing a rally car, because the narrow lanes mean that a fast small car will generally beat a fast big car. Since the rally· car is in a continual drift on the dirt or snow, the smaller the car is the easier it is to keep from smacking the trees. Navigation equipment can be confined to a set of heavy-duty mileage counters; they should be driven from a non-driving wheel (i.e., a front-wheel odo drive on a rear-drive car). This will eliminate errors caused by wheelspin. The best interior lights for the navigator are those from light aircraft because the red light they emit does not bother the driver. The car might also acquire some instrumentation such as a tachometer, oil pressure and temperature gauges, and so forth.

Scott recommends mud and snow tires to help handling and durability on the rough; mileage measurement is not too important because a mileage is given at every action point. He advises some suspension tuning, and some high-performance brake linings and shock absorbers. The engine sump, transmission, and gas tank should all have rock protection, and the exhaust system should be modified to eliminate breakage from vibration. Fuel and brake lines, wiring, and extra lights should all have rock protection. The wiring should be modified to carry the electrical load of the driving lights; circuit breakers or fuses should be provided for every function. The engine should be tuned and modified for maximum performance and durability, and each owner has to pick his own compromise for his rally car. Scott's current rally tool is a Dodge Colt that is equipped with all the modifications he advises and then some. He has high-performance drive train components supplied by Mitsubushi for off-highway use in the U.S.; most imported cars have similar goodies available.

The well prepared stage rally car will eventually be as highly modified as a road racing sedan, but will still be streetable. Some teams, with a good bit of sponsorship, bring in all the engine goodies used on the big-buck European factory teams for their car. A couple of north-central enthusiasts have imported their whole rally car, in this case a rally-prepared Ford Escort. This English car never has been sold in this country, primarily because it was not built to meet current federal laws. By and large, the law enforcers do not bother the special rally cars as long as they are properly muffled and outwardly innocent in appearance. The improved rally car could be a problem in a smog check, but these cars are seldom on the street except during the rally competition. Like any other racer, they are in pieces in the garage most of the time.

The pro series, the POR, the Canadian and Mexican events, and the local bash through the woods are just the spot for the driver who wearies of the mental struggles of TSD work. He must be able to repair things, and he must enjoy crashing about on dirt roads through sand, woods, marshes, and snow in the middle of the night. He should be adept at winching his car out of mudholes and snow banks as well. The navigator's chores on these rallies are less vital to the team effort than are the car's durability and the driver's ability to keep the car together and on the road while running fast.

If you are interested in stage rallying, we should mention that one is not advised to start this type of competition without another means of transportation. While not all SCCA pro rallies are as car-breaking as the Michigan type of bash, there is still the very real possibility of mechanical failure, or of bending the car around a tree or putting it into a ditch. In Michigan the average stage rally loses a good third of the entry for one of these reasons, and the car is then off the road for some time while repairs to car and budget proceed. The owner of a stage rally car should be as ready as the amateur racer to lose both money and the use of the car without strain.

While we do not expect the Pro Rally Series, or any other stage rally, to become as newsworthy in the U.S. as they might be elsewhere in the world, it is still satisfying to see how the 1970s have brought respectability and some recognition to this segment of the sport. It is hard to envision any part of motor sport displacing Texas League baseball in some American newspapers, but the pro series events are at least getting covered by the daily paper in some cities. The 1972 Press-On-Regardless Rally was covered on Detroit television, and the efforts there have aroused a good deal of interest in the sport. The Press-On-Regardless Rally carries the same prestige in the world of rallying as the U.S. Grand Prix at Watkins Glen carries in racing. We expect, as the decade moves forward, that the POR will be joined by a few more FIA-sanctioned rallies around the country, and perhaps the stage rallyist will have a good circuit of FIA-type events to run in preparation for the POR each year.

FIA Championship rallies bring out the top pros, and service crews are necessary for quick repairs. Crews range from friends of the privateer to full blown factory support teams like this Dodge group.

Tips From the Pros

IN ANY KIND OF COMPETITION there is room for improvement—TSD rallying is no exception. The top winners, the champions, are the first to admit that the learning process never ends. However, the first-year rally team can acquire a lot of tricks used by the pros without going through the process of learning by their own mistakes. Each team in every class has its own method of operation, but there are many basic tips that apply well to all types of events and classes. We make no claims of being expert ourselves, and we have won very few rallies in our years in the sport, but we do know a lot of top rally folks and most of them supply advice quite willingly to the serious rallyist.

One man has put it all on paper and he is certainly well qualified. Consequently we will borrow freely from an article published in *Sports Car,* May 1970, called "How to Rally and Win," by Russ (Alligator) Brown. Russ has twice won the SCCA National Championship navigating for Nathan Jones in Class A. The Houston, Texas, based team won top honors nationally in

1968 and again in 1971, and they play the game strictly to win. Russ graciously gave us his full cooperation to borrow from his article; everything in it is written to apply to the SCCA Championship events. However, the majority of the tips also apply to any TSD rally, and we might add that Brown and Jones averaged a second place in over 40 national and divisional rallies following their own advice.

Brown divides his rally tips into three segments: equipment, approach, and gamesmanship. Many rallyists become fairly proficient at the sport, but somehow never quite get into the winning bracket. Sometimes they never know quite why they can't win, and often buy more and more expensive equipment and still have problems. The only reward in the amateur sport is the trophy, so here are a few methods that will help you prepare for the competition and ensure that you will grab some of the big trophies at rally's end.

The first hints fall under the equipment heading, so be sure that your car is prepared for competition and is reliable. Although few Sunday rallies have a tech inspection, do your own, and take care to check the lights, wheels and tires, windshield washers, wipers, and keep the car in a good state of tune. It is a good idea to get a right side rear-view mirror for the navigator. It can be a handy item to use while out-foxing cars trying to pace you, or you can use it to do the same on a following car. (Later in this chapter we tell you how.) Besides, lady navigators can fix their hair without disturbing the set of the driver's mirror. Think about removing the hub caps, even though they do add to your car's good looks. They also cost time if you should have to fix a flat on a TSD section. You should keep the tire-changing tools and spare readily available, not buried under the weekend luggage, and have an action plan that splits the work of changing the tire between the two people on board. It doesn't hurt to practice a tire change in your driveway a few times to get the drill right, for the minute saved by the side of the road may be a minute to the good on your score.

Always be ready for night rallying, even though it is supposed to be a daylight event. Driving lights may not be a necessity, but the interior lighting should be in the car at all times. Poor weather, a late starting number, or emergency reduced average speeds because of weather or other problems can add unexpected time to the rally route. You might spend the last hour on the road in darkness. Keep the navigation lights as a permanent installation, and also keep a flashlight (with fresh batteries) handy inside the car.

The experts all agree that the first bit of add-on equipment should be a reader board for the route instructions. The driver needs to see the instructions, and with the current rash of note instructions to go with the route instructions, no driver can remember all of it; a glance at the center-mounted route sheet will eliminate a lot of conversation. Our own tip to the team who does not have a reader board is quite simple. The navigator, during a lull such as the odo leg, writes every note on the route instructions on pieces of self-adhesive white paper, sold in stationery stores. Then, as each note comes into action, he just sticks that piece of sticky tape on the dash under the driver's line of sight so he can refer to it at each action point. When the note is no longer active, the navigator just rips that piece of information off the dash. Some rallies will have two or more notes working at the same time, along with complicated route instructions, and we like the sticky tape routine for notes even when we have a reader board for the route instructions. A note mentioned just once may carry through several pages of the route instructions, possibly the entire rally, so the extra reminder is handy when your reader board has rolled past that page.

If you run in Class A, the driver should have an odometer he can easily control so that he can keep track of the mileage and timed turns, leaving the navigator free to keep track of time and other tasks.

Russ Brown says to always carry too many maps of the rally area. He told us that on a Flaming Fall National Rally a hard-to-see sign got the majority of the field lost, including himself and Nathan Jones. But Russ and Nathan had been following the course on a map, and they knew from the map that there was only one way to get to the next instruction. They navigated cross-country to pick up the rally and got a zero on the leg, a first in the rally, and their first national championship. On a confidence leg (a long stretch of miles without a route instruction) a map will ease your mind if you are wondering how many times the road you are looking for,

Another breed of pro is the SCCA computer man. National champ Roger Bohl rallied behind a Heuer-made computer of his design in a Ford-sponsored Mustang for two years. Roger and his wife Kathy won the 24-hour Mexican enduro in 1970; they are the only U.S. team to win a Mexican FIA rally overall.

say Highway 6, crosses the rally road; the map can save you an off-course excursion. A compass is a good thing to have, too. If you do get lost, and then find yourself on the map, you might figure that you need only to head south for a few miles to pick up the course again. However you need to know which way is south. It may be dark, or a cloudy day, and you haven't the vaguest idea what your direction of travel is. So a dashboard compass is a dandy investment, and you should buy a good one because you will find use for it on most any rally.

Be over-equipped. Have all the navigational gear that is allowed in your class. If you use factor cards have two sets, or at least know how to figure your own if you lose a card. Carry two Stevens calculators in case you leave one at the lunch stop, or drive away with it on top of the car. Develop the habit of putting the rally gear on the floor of the car when you get out. And try to do all the calculating in the car, not at the restaurant, thus ensuring that all important papers and equipment— like the watches—are *in the car* at all times.

Be sure you know how to use the equipment you have; this is especially important for the navigator. No matter what your methods, practice rally problems at home so you won't panic on the road. If you use a Stevens or a circular slide rule, practice using a 15-percent odo correction factor on average speed changes, and also do average speed exercises that last for more than 10 miles. If you use factor tables, commit to memory all the factors for speeds divisible by five from 10 to 65 mph. If you use a Curta, try running through average speed changes without looking at the device, and also practice add-time work without inadvertently zeroing the Curta. Learn to read the watches at 59 seconds past the minute and read the right minute and, finally, practice recovering the mileage after an off-course excursion without dismay.

Try making convenient holders for all the rally equipment, and develop the type of lap board that works best in your car. Keep the spare equipment handy in the back seat or where it is readily available. Keep the spare timepieces wound and zeroed or on perfect time, and keep the spare counter zeroed also. Be sure the spare Stevens is ready with the center nut loose, or the Curta zeroed. Have plenty of pencils ready, and make sure they're sharpened. Do all these things at home when you have time to check out your equipment and methods calmly. On the rally you won't have any spare time.

With the equipment ready and the team proficient in its use, says Russ Brown, you next work out your methods of operation. First of all, read the generals, read them again, and keep reading them until you can quote them from memory. However, don't depend on memory: keep those pieces of paper handy. Go through the generals and underline, preferably in red, every term that applies on the road. Perhaps circle the whole paragraph, or underline the first sentence—whatever you think will catch your eye. This practice eliminates reading through all the chaff (the tire pressure on the checkout car, where the headquarters motel is located, and so forth) when you need to check a course-following convention on the fly. Russ Brown suggests stripping the generals by scissoring out everything which is not needed on the road. Tape the remainder together in some sort of common-sense order, so it will be handy for ready reference.

A good tip is to know the scoring penalties for the various sins committable on the rally. You wouldn't play football without knowing the points and the penalties, but many rally contestants do not know the difference in penalty between that for a missed checkpoint and the max penalty on the leg. Brown told us that he once blew a rally by running out of a free zone five minutes early and slamming right into a checkpoint. He thought a stop in sight of the control would bring a DNF, so he went into the control and was penalized five minutes for being early. He found out later that stopping in sight of a control carried only a one-minute penalty, and that the five-minute penalty he took on the leg cost him eight places in the rally. Know the scoring penalties.

Help yourself in following the route instructions: use a color code. For instance: a yellow marker over each average speed change, a red circle around each pause, a green circle around each gain, and a brown box around course mileages and mileage turns. This system (some system—you pick your own colors) will provide instant recognition of what to do at the action point on the route instruction sheet. If the rally issues two sets of route instructions per car, as most SCCA nationals do, the driver can mark his sheets with a double underline on the turns and a single underline for signs.

Of course the navigator must keep a log, even in Class C. It helps you learn the game, and figure out the traps. It also helps you recover from an off-course excursion. For starters, you might try writing the mileage to each speed-change and checkpoint right on the route instructions together with your calculated time. From this you can develop a log sheet that works. You need to develop a routine for course-recovery, and learn how to estimate the lost time when you shortcut back to the rally route. It takes practice and some educated guesses, plus a look ahead on the route instructions and the maps to find the spot to rejoin the course. Then using your log and your map, estimate the mileage and do your calculations. Learn to do all this without having to think about the methods.

No matter what problems occur, never give up on a rally if at all possible. Brown relates an occasion where he started a national championship event with a miss and a max on the first two legs on Saturday. He and his partner slugged through a recovery operation and eventually placed in the standings. Recovering from a real mess and then posting some zeros is the toughest test in rallying, but you must keep at the task to become a consistent winner.

The good rallyist never assumes anything, but this is a two-edged blade. When you become relatively good at TSD rallying you often start making hasty assumptions. For example, "This average is 4 mph too fast (or too slow). We must be on the wrong road." Another common assumption is, "That sign isn't the one the rallymaster meant after all." The rallyist on his way up should follow the route instructions to the letter. If you do find yourself off course due to a real error in the instructions the leg will be thrown out from the scoring anyhow. If you assume *nothing,* you may have the pleasure of beating the experts who have tried to outguess the rallymaster.

The rally team should devise a definite and positive division of duties. There should be no giant overlap or, worse, a gap. The team will soon learn how much or how little of the major chores each partner can handle, and then divide the chores so that driver and navigator can both enjoy the competition as well as work toward winning. Brown says that he always tries to win, even in club events, and he suggests that one eliminate all non-vital conversation that could be distracting. Brown even switched his method of giving time checks from "minus 2" to "down 2" to get rid of the extra syllable. He put together a glossary of one-syllable words which trigger instant response from his driver. As an example, you see a control around the curve, and you are down 30 seconds. You might say "Oh Lord, there is a control and we're 30 off, get on it!" which leaves the driver buried in rhetoric and wondering whether to stand on the gas or the brake. Brown's word for this situation is quite simply "Flank!", and he makes up most of the missing seconds.

Do everything possible ahead of time, and most of this is the navigator's work. Suppose you note that after the lunch stop you will go through a town later on the route, and the instructions say "at 90 percent of the posted speed limit." While you wait out your lunch time, make a chart with speeds and factors for 90 percent of every speed from 15 to 65 mph by 5 mph increments, and you will be ready for any posted speed limit without in-car panic-style math. The clue is to read ahead in your free moments, and solve all general math problems before the point of action comes up, if at all possible.

Develop a system of priorities on what should be the most

important moves. Brown describes a loser as a team that comes squealing into an intersection, down two minutes. They have to make an average speed change, a small add-time, and a turn, plus they have several signs to spot, one of which is needed for a coming mileage turn. Five minutes later our losers are absolutely perfectly on-time but heading for the horizon on the wrong road, never to be seen again. The proper sequence is "where" first and "when" second if multiple actions are required or if there just isn't time to do it all. If you are in doubt, stop and look at the signs. A 15-second stop and debate over the rules or how the sign is really spelled can solve a great many problems. Looking doubtfully over the shoulder at the back of a swiftly receding sign or intersection is how to collect big errors on your score.

Be sure to check your in-time on your watch against the time you receive from the control. Brown states that not checking the assigned time is akin to not checking the change from a twenty dollar bill at the local saloon. You must know what time you crossed the in-marker. If there is a discrepancy, you are more apt to win the decision if you have accurate records, and have established a reputation for keeping accurate times. If you have an extra stop watch, run it for each leg and hit it as you cross the in-line. That watch can be like a character witness in court if you are mistimed.

At lunchtime, learn to ignore the inviting-looking restaurant midway through the transit zone. You might enjoy the food there, but it's easy to find yourself just paying the tab when you have two miles left in the transit zone and a half minute to get there. Even if there is enough time, do you want to risk getting lost in a strange town? Transit zone instructions are notorious for their vagueness. So make sure you cover the distance with time to spare. Use the lunch break to gas the car, and then drive to the end of the zone. The non-winners will be enjoying lunch while you eat a sandwich you packed in the car, but chances are you will be getting a trophy at rally's end. Time enough then to eat formally. Arriving early at the end of a transit zone or free zone gives you time to recalculate things, look ahead on the route, and also check your out-time against the surrounding cars. (Timing your neighbor's departure is part of your learning process, which we elaborate on later.)

All the experts advise the serious rallyist to find out what he did wrong on each event. Never leave the finish without understanding why you didn't win. If you got lost, how did you do it? If a trap caught you, learn how and why *this* weekend, instead of falling into the same trap next weekend. Check your log to get your calculated time for each leg; on those legs where it doesn't match the official time, find out why. This is the best possible way to learn the right and wrong of rallying. If you can't figure out what went wrong, ask one of the pros. He'll be so pumped up, he will fall all over himself helping you out. Besides, without your entry fee he probably wouldn't be taking home quite as nice a trophy. A really dedicated rallyist will ask questions until he is satisfied that he knows what caused his downfall. He will even drive back to the area where he goofed and run through the instruction again to see how it all works out properly. Practice in avoiding traps is the only way to gain enough experience to anticipate them on the next rally. There is scarcely a pro in any sport that doesn't practice constantly, and all phases of rally work need some practice. Either practice on your own, or run in some low key events to stay sharp.

However, many rallyists will start a major rally without a bit of warmup, even though they haven't run an event in a month or more. Usually they blow the first few instructions that are tricky. Why not run a Friday night rally the weekend of a big event just to get in shape? If that isn't possible, get up a half hour early on rally day, and practice a few average-speed changes on the highway. Make sure all your equipment works properly. These things are important if you really want to be a consistent winner. Run as many rallies as you can fit into your schedule. Each rally is part of the learning process, and the work will get more and more simple as you gain more and more practice at the problems involved.

Russ Brown is convinced that gamesmanship is a big factor in the winning of an SCCA national. His first piece of advice is to study the rallymaster. Know his style of rally and know whether he writes timing contests or TSD-disguised gimmick events. Know whether he uses traps or plays everything straight. Know if you need to shoot for zeros or if a ten average will win. Brown has files on every active national rally organizer in eight states; he feels that once a rallymaster adopts a style of rally he seldom changes it. This study of the rallymaster works in local rallies too. It usually takes a good year of running to encounter all the top rally organizers on any circuit. You can shortcut a bit just by talking to members of the organizing club prior to the rally. You might find out something about the rallymaster's style by talking to club members about past rallies he has written, even if you haven't run them. His helpers might supply some clues. Just fishing for an estimate on the winning score will tell you whether the rally is a zero contest or one that can be won with a steady drive and a few points on each leg.

The big rallies will publish an entry list, so study the competitors and figure out who is good and who is a mullet. Memorize the color, rally number, type of car, or license number of all vehicles five places in front and behind you. Classify them as expert or mullet. If Milton Mullet, running one car ahead of you, suddenly appears on the road coming toward you at full speed, ignore him. But, if Peter Pro passes looking distraught, you had better check on your own whereabouts. Knowing the entry will help you make an intelligent guess.

You should also know the out-times from the last control of the cars around you. You can usually watch at least two cars ahead of you leave—time them. Write down the differences in time between them and your car; with some practice you can guess the out-time of the car behind as well. Having times ahead and behind, you can establish a tight time frame each leg for use if needed. If you blew some instructions, cut the course, and got back on the route, you can recover by pacing your neighbors, providing you didn't miss a checkpoint. If you find the car that left the last control ahead of you (a pro! you hope), fall in behind it and you will be less than a minute off if he is on time. If this works and the leading car is right on, you can get close to a zero by timing that car through a turn or past a utility pole ahead, and leave that point exactly one minute later. This system can work for a full recovery and a zero. You can also catch a time from the car behind you in the same way. If you are really riding in luck, you can get a forward and a rearward time—two timing references on two different cars for a free recovery from a goof. It is really helpful to get sandwiched between pros. You then have a slick two-minute time zone, provided you stay on course, and you should be able to run less than a minute off no matter what happens to all the gear in the back seat. Just pick carefully the cars you bird dog: you could be led down the garden path also. And when you move into the expert class yourself, you need to watch for hackers just described. If you see a lost mullet storming up course trying to get you in his sights opposite a utility pole or through a turn, back off or speed up as much as possible. It gives the hacker a poor time, and keeps you ahead of the game.

Many rallies today allow the cars to enter the control after a U-turn. In the early days, passing a control backwards was as good as missing it all together on score. If the rally allows U-turns in sight of a control, you can take advantage of that to recover from a max. If you are not more than a minute or so late, at least under the max limit, here is the method. You will usually see the control for some distance because most of them are not concealed from the outbound side. Check the out-marker line as you pass; very often the official time, mileage, or next instruction number is posted there. Also check all the cars in the control as you pass, particularly the one just entering; you may know his out-time from the last leg. With all this information and great luck, you just might figure the proper length U-turn—quick or long—for a good score.

Most pros agree that an early starting number is quite valuable. In a populous area, car number five and all those which follow get noticed by the citizenry. An irate call or two may bring the police to greet car 15. Car 16 and beyond may all max the leg due to the delay. Even without such a drastic problem, cars 5 through 20 will usually pull some kids out of their homes to watch, and the youngsters automatically point out the way the other cars went. But by the time 20 cars have gone by, they may decide to have even more fun by pointing the next bunch of rally cars in the direction the others didn't go—another hazard of a high starting number in an urban area. On the other hand, it isn't a good idea to get car number 1 through 3 either. You don't want to be the one that wakes up the checkpoint people or has the new crew members learn on your time.

Russ Brown suggests that you "do unto others (in other classes) as you would have them do unto you" and be a good sport at all times. Sportsmanship is the name of the game.   **167**

Assistance rendered to someone in another class is like the proverbial bread upon the water, and it is surprising how that assistance comes back double when you need it the most. However, in *your own* class Brown says "do unto others before they do unto you." His gamesmanship ploys include discussing the clever location of checkpoint 15 at the gas stop, when only 14 controls have been encountered on the route. He also likes the bit of stating to another competitor, a few seconds before his out-time comes up on a leg, "Why on earth are you leaving now?" Each team will develop their own little bits of business if they play the rally game that hard, and for some these little ploys are half the fun of rallying among the pros.

Our own observations confirm these tips from the pros, and we have a couple of our own. The first is no gimmick and it's so simple that its value might be underestimated: join a rallying club. We think any serious rallyist should join a rallying club. Work on the checkpoints, run checkout, experience the full spectrum of rally activity. You will find that your competitive skills will increase and you will meet a great many new friends who share your interest in rallying. The association with other rally types at all levels of ability will sustain your interest in the sport also. Besides, competiton is always more fun when you are running for club team trophies as well as for the individual honors.

Our best tip for the improving rallyist is, after joining the club, ask for expert help on the things that give you the most trouble. It would be ideal to run a rally with an expert driver or navigator on a Friday night event or a club rally. We have learned more about the rally game driving or navigating for an expert, using his equipment setup, than we ever have in years of fogging about by ourselves. Nothing can replace experience on the road, and having an expert at your elbow to explain why you are making the moves you are making is tops in our book. The expert can clarify many things in the generals as they come up on the road, and the traps in the route instructions will be explained away with all the signs in full view as you pass. One ride with an expert will teach you as much as a half dozen rallies on your own.

Naturally, nothing can ensure your win, because you need a driver who is quick as a cat, has at least six eyes, and is part of the car. The navigator will have to be a hardy mathematical-law expert. But two ordinary people can acquire all this through practice. Use these suggestions, and with some time and practice on the rally trails you will be carrying home more trophies than you care to keep dusted.

15

The Future of Rallying

RALLYING has evolved over the last 25 years to a unique contest in this country, and it is growing in scope as well as in participation all over the nation. Not only do sports car groups rally, but so do motorcyclists, and four-wheel-drive enthusiasts, and dune buggy people. It seems that the whole motorized community is rallying these days. Rallying is one of the few forms of motorsport that is competitive but not highly expensive, and thousands of people enjoy it.

We are optimistic about the future of all pleasure motoring, despite predictions of doom for the private automobile and our present life style. We feel that rallying is the more likely segment of motor sport to survive in the era of safe and low polluting passenger cars. Because all-out speed is not the essence of most rallies, the heavier, low performance car will be far more competitive in a rally than it will be on the race course.

The average rally car is a compact or import model, and it tends to get better than average fuel economy. This factor could be important for the future of rallying in days of fuel shortages.

Many clubs put on an annual economy run, which is a rally where the score is decided by accurate time and the best gas mileage in ratio to car weight (called ton mileage). Usually the cars are weighed on a truck scale prior to the start. Economy run rallies were really popular a few years back, brought into life by the nationwide publicity given to the annual Mobil Economy Run. The Mobil Economy run was a cross-country rally, often coast to coast, sponsored by the oil company and open to manufacturer's teams, but limited to current-model American-built cars. There was just one overall elapsed time for each day, but you did have to calculate town speeds and highway speeds for your particular vehicle in relation to its fuel economy curve and still make the time schedule at the end of the day. Mobil dropped the promotion in 1968, but we think such an event today, with major oil company sponsorship, would be a demonstration of fuel economy in the present crop of emission-controlled cars, both foreign and domestic. It seems natural for some company which is pushing low-lead or no-lead gas to organize an economy run rally as a means of proving that their fuel is as good as leaded gas in the modern car, maybe even prove the dreaded catalytic mufflers. There are numerous applications of this type of rally for commercial sponsorship.

Any cross country event, be it border-to-border or coast-to-coast, has a great appeal to the press, and we think a cross-country rally should be part of the American motoring scene. For instance, the press coverage given to the Cannonball Baker Sea-to-Shining-Sea Memorial Trophy Dash in recent years is well out of proportion to the importance of the event to the average person. But it has the charm of long distance running and competing on public highways, albeit illegally, and it seems to be great fun for the contestants. However, as much as we enjoy racing, we prefer to do that on a closed and designated course, and use the public roads for rallying only. Common sense dictates that any major event of this nature needs the full cooperation of law enforcement agencies.

In the future we expect to see some long-distance rallies in this country, and we expect sponsored events that will probably be organized by the Sports Car Club of America, simply because they have a nationwide network of regions to handle local checkpoints and other logistics. Presently, the point system each year determines the SCCA national champions in both the National Rally Series and the Pro Series. It would not be impossible to have a runoff rally for the national championship. National Rally Board Member Frank Schmitz, of Kansas City, suggested this runoff business several years ago. He organized a two-day event in the Midwest Division as a prototype, but Ford's four-car Mustang team was exhibiting such dominance in the national point series that interest in either the series or a run-off was at low ebb. Still, using the divisional system from amateur racing, the SCCA could nominate six or more teams from each division for entry in a runoff rally, which would provide a heads-up battle for at least 42 cars for the national championship. Of course such an event would need a sponsor. It could be a three-day event, with each day's rally done by a different rallymaster from a different part of the country. To simplify the logistics, the headquarters area would remain the same.

Another method of doing a runoff rally is a bit more involved on logistics, but far more fascinating. It would be a Monte Carlo rally, in which each entry would rally from his home city to a common meeting area in the middle of the country. Then there could be two more days of TSD rallying with the total point score establishing the new national champions.

In the performance or driver's-rally field, we long for the return of the dirt road Trans—Canada run, and for a North American series involving Canada, the U.S., Mexico, Puerto Rico and Jamacia, all with big FIA rallies each year. We have often thought that a cross country Tour de France style rally would work beautifully in the U.S. The Tour de France for automobiles was quite simply an elapsed-time rally that ran for days from race course to race course all over France. The rally sections were quite simple, and the performance of car and driver was tested in relative safety at proper race courses. Naturally the race track performance was the deciding factor in the win. This type of thing could be easily done and be done quite legally in America, and it might encourage manufacturers from all ends of the earth to enter and prove the superiority of their products.

Even if the cross-country events should come into existence, we think the time-speed-distance rally will remain the backbone of the sport in this country, and we also think that the local club event will endure as the heartland of rallying. Most rally people seldom venture beyond local events; they have no desire to trek all over the country in search of trophies. They rally for fun and for the competition. Even experts feel that way. Many top experts never go points-searching beyond their local council of clubs. So you can stay home and have fun!

Fun is what rallying is all about, and, although rallying has its ups and downs in numbers of contestants, we see the sport gaining participants in the years to come. We do not believe that this generation, or the next, will part with the private automobile altogether. And as long as that is true there will be rallying—just for fun.

RESOURCES

RALLY PUBLICATIONS

THE RALLYIST (monthly)
344 Monte Vista Avenue, No. 2E
Oakland, California 94611

SPORTS CAR NEWS (monthly)
Long Island Sports Car News
P.O. Box 167
Glen Oaks, New York 11004

THE STOPWATCHER (monthly)
4522 Amherst Lane
Bethesda, Maryland 20014

ROAD AND TACH (monthly)
Santa Monica Sports Car Club
2627 Midvale Avenue
Los Angeles, California 90064

PAMPHLETS AND OTHER INFORMATION

SPORTS CAR CLUB OF AMERICA, INC.
Rally Director, P.O. Box 22476
Denver, Colorado 80222

PRESS ON REGARDLESS RALLY
8988 Tavistock Court
Plymouth, Michigan 48170

ST. VALENTINE'S DAY MASSACRE
P.O. Box 212,
Flossmoor, Illinois 60422

SPORTS CAR PRESS (rally tables)
Sylvester Court
East Norwalk, Connecticut 06855

PIRELLI TIRE CORPORATION
60 East 42nd Street
New York, New York 10017

DATSUN RALLY HEADQUARTERS
P.O. Box 191
Gardena, California 90247

HEUER TIME CORPORATION
(Guide to Rally Timing)
960 South Springfield
Springfield, New Jersey 07081.

MAJOR RETAIL OUTLETS FOR RALLY EQUIPMENT

ARITROL (computer)
6511 East Lincoln Drive
Paradise Valley, Arizona 85253

COMPETITION LTD. (general)
23840 Leland
Dearborn, Michigan 48124

FELDMAR WATCH CO. (timers)
9002 West Pico Boulevard
Los Angeles, California 90035

VILEM B HAAN, INC. (Halda etc.)
11401 West Pico Boulevard
West Los Angeles, California 90064

MG MITTEN (general)
36 South Chester
Pasadena, California 91106

RALLECOMP (computer and Rodon
electronic clock)
P.O. Box 1787
Costa Mesa, California 92626

STEVENS ENGINEERING CO.
(odos, etc.)
340 North Newport Boulevard
Newport Beach, California
92660

BURNS INDUSTRIES (Curta etc.)
361 Delaware Avenue
Buffalo, New York 14202

DENCO (general)
Box 5303
Spokane, Washington 99205

F & W RALLYE ENGINEERING
(general)
P.O. Box 143
Utica, Michigan 48087

JOSLIN COMPUTER CO.
(Autonav)
P.O. Box 90153
Los Angeles, California 90009

RALLY INTERNATIONAL
(general; Zeron computer distributor)
370 East 134th Street
New York, New York 10454

SHEETZ-GULL (computer
readout)
6716 Bostwick Drive
Springfield, Virginia 22151

WHITMORE ELECTRONICS CO.
(rally computer)
410 Northwest 117th Street
Miami, Florida 33168

Editor   Ed Reading
Designer   Hal Crippen
Art Assistant   Sonja Keith

CPSIA information can be obtained
at www.ICGtesting.com
Printed in the USA
LVOW07*1522180917
549130LV00007B/79/P

9 780393 600025